BARMY

Jack Crossley spent some ~~40 years~~ first as a reporter on the *Daily Mail* and later as news editor/assistant editor on the *Mail*, the *Observer*, the *Herald* (Glasgow), the *Daily Express*, *The Times* and, for two crazy months, the *National Enquirer* in Florida.

He also edited the *Sunday Standard*, a short-lived quality broadsheet in Scotland, and was briefly a reporter on the Quincy *Patriot Ledger* in Massachusetts.

He is now retired – sort of – but still regularly provides news and investigation ideas to newspapers and magazines. Jack lives in London with his wife, Kate, and they spend much of their time fishing and messing about in boats on the Thames at Henley and off the coast of Cornwall.

BARMY
BRITAIN

Published by John Blake Publishing Ltd,
3 Bramber Court, 2 Bramber Road,
London W14 9PB, England

www.johnblakepublishing.co.uk

First published in paperback in 2008

ISBN 978 1 84454 682 4

British Library Cataloguing-in-Publication Data:

A catalogue record for this book is available from the British Library.

Design by www.envydesign.co.uk

Printed and bound in Great Britain by Creative Print & Design,
Blaina, Wales

1 3 5 7 9 10 8 6 4 2

Papers used by John Blake Publishing are natural, recyclable
products made from wood grown in sustainable forests.
The manufacturing processes conform to the environmental
regulations of the country of origin.

**BIZARRE-BUT-TRUE STORIES
FROM ACROSS THE NATION**

BARMY
BRITAIN

JACK CROSSLEY

JOHN BLAKE

To my son Gary

CONTENTS

INTRODUCTION

Having spent over half a century working on newspapers, I am still well-placed to plough through chaotic piles of newsprint and magazines, searching for the ridiculous and offbeat and decidedly British. I started as a 14-year-old copy boy on the *Yorkshire Evening News* in Leeds and then went to the *Daily Dispatch* in Manchester, followed by a six month holiday relief stint at the *Daily Mail*'s Manchester office: the perfect training ground to identify and make a note of stories that embrace our traditional role of triumphantly meddling through with affable incompetence.

Some of the items which make up this book take no more than a couple of minutes to note down; others can take half an hour or more – digesting long articles and extracting from them a couple of sentences that throw some light on what it is about the British that make the British British.

I would like to thank the publications listed at the end of this book. But most of all, I would like to thank every eccentric character whose antics have ensured their appearance between these covers. Bravo Barmy Britain!

CHAPTER 1

SIGNS OF THE TIMES

Drivers advised to 'Honk if you like our quiet town'...

Spotted on the back of a motorcyclist:

IF YOU CAN READ THIS
MY WIFE FELL OFF.

Independent on Sunday

Due to an error in transmission we reported that a lady was found dead with a bottle in her hand. This should have read 'bible'.

Swindon Evening Advertiser

Simon Heffer tells of the effect of a superstore opening outside his market town. It was summed up by a notice put up by a local fishmonger: 'Please do not mention Tesco, as a smack in the mouth often offends'.

Daily Telegraph

A shop sign advertised 'Extra Large Bonsai Trees'.

Independent

W. George Preston of Southampton spotted for sale a 'Jumbo Mini Fan'.

Daily Telegraph

Johnson and Johnson's rectal thermometer comes with the guarantee that 'All Johnson and Johnson's products are personally tested'.

Kelvin Mackenzie, the *Sun*

Dave and Anne Osborn of Fettercairn, Laurencekirk, spotted this sign:

BELL NOT WORKING
OPEN DOOR AND SHOUT

Daily Mail

Richard Bird, of Blewbury, Oxfordshire, says he has been kept amused for years by a large digital display road sign he once saw. On a support pole at the side of the road there was a sign saying: 'This sign is not yet in use'.

Independent

Ian Hall, of Burnhill Green, South Staffordshire, writes in *The Times* about a notice at an entrance to self-catering accommodation he saw in Cork, Ireland:

'To operate the security lock, press buttons 2 and 4 together then press 3. If you still can't open the door, the one at the end of the corridor is not locked.'

The Times

K. J. Faulks, of Leicester, spotted this classified ad in the *Leicester Mercury*:

'Computer wooden gas operated, good condition £30'.

Leicester Mercury

Robert Price of Penrith, Cumbria, tells of his new power jigsaw with its mains lead, electric motor, sharp blades and a laser. The instructions came in a plastic bag bearing the warning: 'Plastic bags can be extremely dangerous'.

The Times

Sign in a Portsmouth shopping centre: 'Illegal parking enforced'.

Independent

Miss M. L. Whittle, of Bournemouth, asks 'Couldn't they just clamp them?' after reading this notice in a café/shop in Kimmeridge, Dorset:

ANY CARS PARKED IN THIS CAR PARK WHOSE OWNERSHIP WE ARE UNABLE TO ASCERTAIN BY ENQUIRY WITHIN OUR PREMISES WILL BE DONATED TO THE MOD GUNNERY SCHOOL FOR TARGET PRACTICE

Daily Mail

A pre-paid Business Reply Service envelope bears the address:

Post Office Savings, PO Box 198, Widnes, WA8 2AA

On the back there is this message:

If undelivered return to: Post Office Savings, PO Box 198, Widnes, WA8 2AA.

Colin Stonely, *Independent on Sunday*

Well-behaved Dogs and Children Welcome on Leads' – advert for the Turfcutters Arms in the *Waterside Herald*, spotted by Mrs Brenda Stevens, Southampton.

Waterside Herald

BUYING or SELLING a house could cost you dear. See a SOLICITOR... Just to be SURE.

Yorkshire Evening Press

Seen on a car in Norfolk: 'If you can read this where the hell is my caravan?'

G. Wilford, King's Lynn, Norfolk. *Daily Telegraph*

Notice in a London restaurant menu: 'There is a very small possibility of finding nuts in our dishes that do not contain them at all.'

F. W. Crawley, London N6. *The Times*

I noticed that my 'vanilla flavour' yoghurt listed 14 added ingredients – not one of which was vanilla.

Ian Sykes, *The Times*

Seen in the back window of a van: 'I owe, I owe, so off to work I go'.

Susan Morris, Chalfont St Peter.
Reader's Digest

'Neuter your cat at a cut price'. Ad in the Derby *Evening Telegraph*.

Jack Phillips, Derby. *Daily Mail*

Nigel Stapley, of Brymbo, Wrexham, recalls his favourite newspaper correction: 'Due to a mishearing on the telephone we reported that Mr and Mrs (name withheld) would be living with the bride's father. They will in fact be living at the Old Manse.'

Guardian

'Virgin sleepers. Never been laid. £18 each plus VAT.'
Advertisement quoted in the *Guardian*

An advert for a pets' underskin microchipping service, seen in a local paper in Droitwich, Worcestershire: '£9.50 per animal. Pensioners free'.

Daily Mail

Notice in a memorabilia shop in Mevagissey, Cornwall: 'Do not tell the shopkeeper that you used to have one of those at home'.

Metro

The instructions with my new steam iron includes the warning: 'Never steam iron the garment you are wearing'.
Christopher Bell, Sevenoaks, Kent. *The Times*

I recently bought a pack of tablets that states on the container: 'For the relief of headaches'. Among the list of possible side effects it says: 'May cause headaches'.
Ken Battersby, Millom, Cumbria. *Daily Telegraph*

I have been given a prescription for a medicine that has 83 possible side-effects, none of which I have suffered in the past. It would seem the cure is more hazardous than the complaint.

Ken Hill, Farnborough, Hants. *Daily Telegraph*

Inflatable single mattress, complete with pump. Ideal for those unwanted guests.

Advert in *Basildon Evening Echo. Sunday Times*

'Visitors are invited to bring along some food suitable for sharing in a finger buffet'.

From the *Swindon Evening Advertiser* announcing a talk by missionaries on cannibalism.

'If you enjoy working with people, why not become a mortuary technician?'

Dorset Echo

On a recent car journey we passed a fitness centre with the banner: 'Detox Here'. A mile or two further on there was a pub sign: 'Retox Here'.

Elaine Brooksbank, Illingworth, West Yorskshire. *Reader's Digest*.

Instructions on a new digital telephone include: 'When the other person answers, speak'.

Debbie Beasley, Langdon Hills, Essex. *The Times*

Sir, I recently borrowed an aluminium extending ladder and, having climbed to the top, I found a small bright orange sticker with an arrow pointing at the top rung. In French, German and English it read: 'STOP! This is the last rung'. I wonder who would ignore this instruction and carry on?

Les Wayles of Christchurch, Dorset.
The Times

In a contest to find Britain's silliest packaging instructions the samples below were finalists:

- Nytol sleep aid: 'Warning: may cause drowsiness'.
- Tesco's Tiramisu dessert: 'Do not turn upside down' – printed on bottom of box.
- Marks and Spencer's bread pudding: 'Product will be hot after heating'.
- Boots Children's Cough Medicine: 'Do not drive a car or operate machinery after taking this medication'.
- On several brands of Christmas lights: 'For indoor or outdoor use only'.
- On irons: 'Never iron clothes on the body'.
- On Lip Enhancing Gloss: 'For external use on the oral lips only'.
- On a child's Superman costume: 'Wearing this garment does not enable you to fly'.

Sunday Telegraph

Found on the underside of a box of sweets; 'Do not read while the carton is open'.

Chris Spurrier, Hampshire. *The Times*

A woman writes from America to tell the Daily Telegraph about the Harry Potter broomstick given to her five-year-old. The packaging read: 'Caution. Broom does not really fly.'

Daily Telegraph

On the handlebars of a child's scooter: 'Caution. This product moves when used.'

Martin G. Sexton, Norwich. *The Times*

Sign advertising rabbits outside a butcher's shop in Worthing, West Sussex:

WATERSHIP DOWN.
YOU'VE READ THE BOOK.
YOU'VE SEEN THE FILM.
NOW TRY THE STEW.

Yorkshire Evening Post

Sign in a Chelsea butcher's window:

> YOU'VE READ THE BOOK. YOU'VE SEEN THE FILM. NOW EAT THE CAST.

Jennifer North, London SW1V. *The Times*

My favourite sign was in the window of an Indian restaurant in the Midlands: 'Once you have eaten here, you'll recommend others.'

Maggie D'Araujo, Bristol.
Guardian

Sign on a car park exit machine in Mousehole on the Cornish coast:

> IF THE BARRIER FAILS TO OPERATE, GIVE THE MACHINE A LIGHT TAP. IF IT IS STILL NOT WORKING, PLEASE CALL AT THE SECOND SHOP ON THE LEFT AS YOU ENTER THE VILLAGE. IF THE SHOP IS CLOSED, CONTACT MR. SMITH AT 7 NEW ROAD, MOUSEHOLE.

R. D. Nash, St. Ives, Cornwall.
Daily Mail

Wacky warning labels have included: 'Do not allow children to play in the dishwasher.' 'This wood drill is not intended for use as a dental drill.' 'Remove child before folding this push chair.' 'Never iron clothes while they are being worn.'

Independent on Sunday

I once stayed in a Blackpool B&B featuring a sign reading: 'No Wearing Boots in Bed.'

Andrew Marr, *Daily Telegraph*

The packaging on a rain gauge purchased by David Booker of Bognor Regis carried the words: 'Ideal for outdoors'.

The Times

On leaving the M5 and taking the road to Portishead there's a sign saying: 'Danger – Low Flying Owls'. On the A249 in Kent there is signpost for Hucking on which someone has written underneath: 'Hell'.

Daily Mail

There was a demonstration of marital arts on the village green.

Spotted by Bob Lee of Byfleet, Surrey in the Byfleet and Addlestone Review. Daily Mail

John Furniss, of Bedale, North Yorkshire, bought sunglasses with a label saying that they were 'Filter Category 1, tested to British Standard BS EN1836'. A second label said: 'Not for use in bright sunlight'.

The Times

A *Daily Telegraph* reader saw a birthday card for an 80-year-old that carried the message: 'Not suitable for children under three'. Ricky Kelehar, of London N16 then wrote to say he had bought a card with the same message. Unfortunately it was for a two-year-old.

Daily Telegraph

Luton Angling Club has designed a sign showing a swan inside a red circle along with a knife and fork and the *Guardian* asks: Does it mean 'Don't Feed the Swans?' Or 'Swans Not Served Here?' Or 'A Swan Is Never To Be Used As Cutlery?' Apparently the sign is aimed at informing immigrants that wild swans are not for human consumption – 'Unless you are the Queen, who eats them every Wednesday.'

Guardian

The Bennetts of Pilton, Somerset, sent their daughter a 'Congratulations on Your Graduation' card. On the reverse it said: 'Not suitable for children under five.'

The Times

Claire-Marie Slater, of Tunbridge Wells, bought a disposable barbecue with this warning: 'Do not use in cribs, beds, prams or playpens.'

The Times

Bryan Flake writes about passing through a quaint village with this greeting sign:

'HONK IF YOU LIKE OUR
QUIET LITTLE TOWN'.

Reader's Digest

Sign seen at Unst, Shetland Isles, by Mrs M Featherstone, of Spalding, Lincolnshire:

DONALD RITCH
PURVEYOR OF
FINE MEATS,
FLAT CAPS
& TURPENTINE

Daily Mail

This road sign was spotted by Robert Kite, of Sutton-in-Ashfield, Nottinghamshire:

> **BROADBOTTOM**
> **PUBLIC CONVENIENCES**

'Where do the narrow bottoms go?' asked the caption.
Daily Mail

As part of its determination to get tough on crime a police force put up signs urging: 'Don't Commit Crime'. Other daft signs spotted by the Plain English Campaign included:
- Water on Road During Rain
- All Fuel Must be Paid For (at petrol stations)
- Warning! Platform Ends Here (at a railway station)

Sun

Seen in an Edinburgh bar:

> **EAT HERE & YOU'LL NEVER**
> **LIVE TO REGRET IT**

Spotted by Mr R. Howard, of Manchester. *Daily Mail*

Pauline Moore of Woodbridge, Suffolk, reports a birthday card bearing the message: 'May this be your best birthday ever'. It was for a one-year-old.

Sunday Telegraph

Seen on a fence in the Lake District near Crummock Water and photographed by Peter Pedley:

> **TEK CARE**
> **LAMBS ONT ROAD**

Seen on a farm gate at Cockerham, near Lancaster, by Malcolm Nightingale, of Preston, Lancashire:

> **OWER SHEEP AVE NO**
> **ROAD SENSE**

Daily Mail

CHAPTER 2
SPORTING LIFE

Sporting joy sweeps through England after victories in three major sports – football, rugby, and... conkers...

A box containing a pair of Puma trainers carries this vital information: 'Average Contents: Two'.

Daily Mail

Brighton and Hove Albion are blessed with a diminutive mid-fielder, Dean Cox – inspiring some fans to chant: 'We've got tiny Cox'. Others prefer: 'We've got five-foot Cox'.

Guardian

The *Guardian* followed this up, recalling how Bristol City had a manager called Alan Dicks, who had to endure the howl: 'Dicks out!'

Guardian

The weekend of 20–21 October 2007 kicked off with British hopes of world championships on two fronts. But Formula One boy racer Lewis Hamilton lost his chance of becoming world champion and the England rugby team were runners up in the World Cup. As *The Times* reported: 'Many will see this as a disastrous weekend for British sport, but it is nothing of the sort... Look at it this way: It's not that England lost, it's that they nearly won.'

The Times

Fiery fast bowler Freddie Trueman saw a batsman flick one of his balls towards fielder Raman Subba Row. But the balled slipped through the fielder's hands and then through his legs. Subba Row apologised and said: 'I should have kept my legs shut.'

'Aye, lad,' said Fred, 'and so should your mother.'

Independent

England cricketer Freddie Flintoff was reported 'to have disgraced himself by getting drunk and absconding on a pedalo'. Jan Moir in the *Daily Telegraph* commented: 'Perhaps this is just another symptom of the strange transformation that comes over many Englishmen when travelling abroad. Freddie was only reverting to national stereotype, so let us not judge him too harshly.'

Daily Telegraph

In his book, More Than a Game, cricket loving former Prime Minister John Major writes of a match between Kent and Essex played at Tilbury Fort.

A Kent player shot and killed a member of the opposing team, a spectator was bayoneted and a soldier shot dead.

Mercifully, it was in 1776.

Sun

Great sporting joy swept throughout England in October 2007 with victories in three major sports – football, rugby and... conkers. 'What a triple triumph!' crowed the Sun – 'normally we'd only expect to win at conkers.'

Sun

At a time when all the other news columns were moaning about how fat everybody is, the Guardian magazine pointed out that some of history's most significant figures have been fat.

Its list includes Henry VIII, Buddha, Father Christmas, Orson Welles, Oliver Hardy and Luciano Pavarotti, and it has this to say of W. G. Grace (a fine all-round cricketer in every sense): 'It's fair to assume that were he playing now, instead of our totally useless current crop, England would still be in the World Cup.'

Guardian G2

Cardiff University gathered together the ecological impact of the 73,000 who attended the Manchester v Millwall FA Cup Final at the city's Millennium Stadium in 2004.

- 37,624 sausage rolls, pies and pasties
- 26,965 sandwiches
- 17,998 hot dogs
- 12,780 burgers
- 11,502 packets of crisps
- 23,909 portions of chips
- 303,001 pints of lager
- 66,584 pints of beer
- 38,906 pints of cider
- 12,452 bottles of wine
- 90,481 shots
- 63,141 alcopops

The binge left its mark on Cardiff city centre:

- 37 tonnes of glass
- 8 tonnes of paper
- 11 tonnes of uneaten food

None was recycled.

Guardian

Some changes needed to be made when The Dangerous Book for Boys was rewritten for the American market. Conkers don't get a mention, but there's something called 'stickball'. You won't find the laws of cricket, but there is the equally incomprehensible Navajo Code Talkers' Dictionary. A section listing the Kings and Queens of England and Scotland has been replaced with The Most Valuable Players in Baseball.

The Times

In England we would call Former Prime Minister the Rt. Hon Sir John Major, KG, something of a cricket anorak. He unashamedly admits that if he knew he was going to die tonight he would still want to know the close-of-play scores. He says: 'Cricket helped to bind the British Empire together.'

Clem Attlee used to get updates of county scores during Cabinet meetings.

The Times

In May 2007 it was reported that Filton Golf Club, near Bristol, had finally ended its 88-year war with Germany and Austria.

In 1919 they thought they would teach them a lesson for starting World War I and banned them from using their course. Now members have decided to let bygones be bygones and rescinded the ban.

Independent on Sunday

The £400,000 London Olympics logo provoked howls of protest and Guardian diarist Jon Henley reported: 'If one more reader emails to tell us that the internet is buzzing with reports that it looks like Lisa Simpson performing an unmentionable act on Bill Clinton, we will scream.'

Guardian

Another critic said: 'To me it represents two drunks trying to help each other up off the ground. Very British, indeed.'
Daily Telegraph

The Rev John Fairweather-Tall of Plymouth, Devon, wrote: 'I saw the logo on your front page. Ought this not to have been on the back page, along with the other puzzles?'

Daily Telegraph

Wars raged and world leaders gathered at the G8 Summit, but British newspapers know what their readers want to know about: 'Changing climate puts World Conker Championship Title in Danger' was a Page One headline in the Daily Telegraph on Monday, 11 June 2007.
Daily Telegraph

Manchester United extended the car park at its training ground to accommodate players'oversized limos.

Independent on Sunday

Eddie the Eagle finished last in the 1988 Winter Olympics in Calgary and was hailed as 'a very British kind of hero'. The *Independent on Sunday* produced some rules on just what it takes to win the affection of the British public and included:

- At all costs don't win. The longer 'Tiger' Tim Henman went without reaching a Wimbledon final the more we took him to our hearts.
- Acquire underdog status. A classic case is cricketer Monty Panesar – wildly enthusiastic and only vaguely athletic. Every wicket Monty takes becomes its own joyful 'would you believe it' story.

Independent on Sunday

'Plant was rooted to the spot.'
Football match report in the *Littlehampton Gazette*.

British newspapers and magazines do their best to maintain the myth that cricket is a gentleman's game. The magazine *Chap* gives this advice for 'keeping the gentleman's game on a decent wicket: 'When batting one should aim mainly to retain one's dignity, particularly at the moment when your wicket is lost. The number of runs you score should be finely balanced so that you do not demoralise the opposition.'

Chap magazine

Foreign visitors to the sacred Lords cricket ground in London can buy an explanation of the game which says:

'You have two sides. One out in the field and one in. Each man that's in the side that's in goes out and when he's out he comes in and the next man goes in until he's out. When they are all out the side that's out comes in and the side that's been in goes out and tries to get those coming in out. Sometimes you get men still in and not out. When both sides have been in and out – including the not outs – that's the end of the game. Howzat!'

From a tea-towel bought at Lords

Leeds manager Eddie Gray: 'It was always an uphill task for us and after they scored it was downhill all the way. It left us with a mountain to climb.'

Sun

A golf ball that stuck in the mouth of a lioness at Knowsley safari park has changed the rules of the game. The game's governing body now says that any golfer who hits a ball into the mouth of a lioness should be allowed to drop another ball on the nearest spot that is not dangerous.

Sunday Times

BBC commentator Kenneth Wolstenholme became a national institution after uttering the most famous words in British sport. As England scored a last-minute fourth goal in their 1966 World Cup triumph over Germany, he announced: 'They think it's all over, it is now.' The *Sun* seized the opportunity of recalling other famous sporting quotes:

- 'Football isn't a matter of life and death – it's much more important than that.' Bill Shankly, manager of Liverpool.
- 'Winning doesn't really matter as long as you win.' Soccer star Vinnie Jones.
- 'For the benefit of those watching in black and white, Tottenham Hotspurs are playing in yellow.' TV commentator John Motson.
- 'Don't tell those just coming in the result of this fantastic match – but let's have another look at Italy's winning goal.' TV commentator David Coleman.

Sun

'Authorities are reluctant to ban bungee jumping in case they drive it underground.'

Radio 4, reported in a letter to the *Guardian*

Henry Longhurst used to say that golf needed only three rules: the player who won the last hole tees off first. The player furthest from the flag putts first. The player who wins stands the first round of drinks.

Letter to *The Times*.

'Wimbledon has changed from being a genteel sports fortnight for the suburban middle classes to a coarse gladiatorial contest for the vulgar masses... but the tennis is better than ever. Buy earplugs.' Philip Howard in *The Times*.

Philip recalled Wimbledon's original official announcements, which included: 'Please do not applaud a double fault.'

The Times

A rugby scrum is 'essentially a boxing match for 16 people without the Queensbury rules. It is home to punching, gouging and testicle twisting. Not pretty.'

Guardian

A Leicester angler uses jelly babies as bait and says that cod like black ones and bass like green ones.

The Times

Falcon Rovers striker Gary Davenport, aged 27, of West Sussex, was banned from the penalty box after heading 14 own goals.

Sun

Somebody may well have said something similar before, but Hugh Muir quotes George Best as saying: 'I spent 90% of my money on women, drink and fast cars. The rest I wasted.'

Guardian Diary

Women now make up to a fifth of all fans attending Premiership football matches – and they enjoy abusing the ref as much as men. They seem to enjoy the singing and the tribalism – and swearing is just as prevalent as it has always been.

Independent on Sunday

Not many Olympic gold medals get pinned onto British chests, but the *Sun* attempted to cheer up its readers by reminding them that 'We're the world champs at wacky sports including gurning (pulling ugly faces), toe wrestling, lawn mower racing, arm wrestling, elephant polo, tug of war, kite-flying, welly-tossing, cheese rolling, black pudding throwing, ferret racing and tiddlywinks.'

Sun

The English rugby team's defeat did not appear to dampen their spirits for their trip home. Their British Airways flight took off with 76 extra bottles of champagne and an increase of 60% in the usual beer allocation.

The Times

On BBC TV a doyen of the snooker table, approaching his 70th birthday, was said to be 'too old to get his leg over and prefers to use his left hand.' And Alex Higgins was said to be 'suddenly, 7-0 down'.

The girlfriend of soccer star Jermain Defoe got a job at the Foreign Office – advising wannabe WAGs how to behave on overseas trips. 22-year-old Charlotte Meares' advice to Wives and Girlfriends includes:

- Get insured in case you fall off a bar table.
- How to cope with broken finger nails or when your extensions turn green in the pool.
- How to cope with cops after wild partying.
- Always check that your hotel has a beauty parlour.
- How to stay looking your best if you are not taking a personal stylist with you.

Sun

Sporting Brits may often fail to shine at international contests, but that's not so when it comes to eccentric events such as the World Bog Snorkelling Championships.

Joanne Pitchforth, a 35 year-old teacher from Heckmondwike, West Yorkshire, beat an international field of 120 competitors and set a new world record at Llanwrtyd Wells, Mid-Wales. She emerged filthy but triumphant after taking 1 minute 35.18 seconds to complete the two 60-yard lengths of peat bog – beating the previous record of 1 minute 35.46 seconds.

28-seconds is a long time when you are up to your neck in a black bog...

The Times

It must rank as one of the weirdest global spectator sports, with more than 1.5million people logging on to watch a 44lb handmade Cheddar cheese from Shepton Mallet slowly maturing. The Somerset-based cheese, named Wedginald, is the star of www.cheddarvisiontv.com. Along with a huge picture of the prized cheese, the website's only other noticeable feature is a chronicle of how long it has been maturing: in days, hours, minutes and seconds.

The Times

Amidst all the fever of the 2007 Rugby World Cup semi finals in October the *Daily Telegraph* had a whole page headlined 30 REASONS WHY WE HATE THE FRENCH. High up on the list:

• Because they make love more than anyone else.
• On average that's 137 times a year.
• We manage only 119.

Daily Telegraph

A *Daily Telegraph* leader said of the rugby that it was a noble defeat which should be inspiring to every Briton.

Daily Telegraph

The *Sun* tried to cheer up its readers with a page one headline:

OH WELL, THERE'S ALWAYS DARTS

Sun

Discussion about New Zealand rugby players performing their pre-match Haka war dance produced the suggestion that the English team should respond with Morris dancing. Peter Croft, of Cambridge, thought that such a response would fall foul of international human rights conventions prohibiting cruel and unusual punishment.

Sunday Telegraph

CHAPTER 3

LAW AND DISORDER

It is illegal to die in the Houses of Parliament...

A woman arrested for shoplifting had a whole salami in her knickers. She said it was because she was missing her Italian boyfriend.

Manchester Evening News

Isobel Whatrup, of Gillingham, Kent, tells of a friend who decided to sell some surplus vegetables from a table outside the house, relying on an honesty box. Someone stole the table.

Daily Telegraph

Karim Allison, of Middlesbrough, reported his wheelie bin missing and got a letter from Victim Support offering him emotional support.

'What I need,' he said, 'is just a new bin.'

Guardian

A set of traffic lights was stolen in Reading and police said: 'Some thieves will stop at nothing.'

Southend Evening Echo

A life-sized cardboard cut-out policeman – set up as a crime prevention measure – was stolen from a supermarket in Ripon, North Yorkshire.

Daily Telegraph

It seems to be becoming a national pastime. Shortly after the above theft another cardboard policeman failed to deter thieves – this time in Long Eaton, Derbyshire. The life-size figure of PC Bob Molloy, who had previously been credited with keeping shoplifters away from the local Co-Op, was seen on CCTV being carried away – tucked under a man's arm.

Sunday Times

The law banning anyone from dying in the Houses of Parliament topped a poll on Britain's most absurd rules. Second was the one banning the sticking of a postage stamp upside-down. More than half of the 3,931 taking part in the poll admitted breaking the law that bans the eating of mince pies on Christmas Day.

Sun

Some like it hot:
Police closed a street in Soho, London, for three hours amid fears of a chemical attack. But the acrid fumes hanging over the street came from a spicy dip with extra chillies being cooked in a Thai restaurant.

Sunday Times

At Woolwich Crown Court Mr Justice Openshaw asked: 'What is a website?' This joins a list of comments that are forever trotted out in support of the legend of judicial ignorance. The list includes:

- What are the Beatles?
- Who is Gazza?
- What is Linford Christie's lunch box?
- What is a Teletubby?
- What is B&Q?

(Next day the judge said he had played dumb 'to assist the jury' and was seeking an explanation 'in the interests of justice')

The Times

A supermarket till operator in Aberdare, South Wales, overheard a customer say 'Battle of Hastings' as she tapped in her PIN. Using the customer's debit card he tapped 1066 into the store's cash machine and plundered £170.

The Times

Ipswich Crown Court gave a driving instructor a 12-month supervision order and 80 hours unpaid community work after hearing that he had told a 17-year-old girl pupil: 'Your breasts would make a good mobile phone holder.'

Daily Mail

19-year-old Kyle Little was arrested under the Public Order Act for barking at two dogs. His name was cleared in Newcastle Crown Court in a hearing that cost £8,000. Judge Beatrice Bolton said: 'I don't think Section Five of the Public Order Act applies to dogs.'

The dogs' owner said: 'They were not upset by it at all.'

Daily Telegraph

PC 1064 of the Norfolk Constabulary is a local hero in Lithuania and has been awarded a medal for the way he helps Lithuanians over here. The ever-helpful *Guardian* filled a page with the story of PC Gary Pettengell and included vital translations of essential phrases:

- Hello, hello, hello (Labas, labas, labas)
- Move along there please (Vijeok deasi prasau)
- Let's be having you (Kilosek minas)
- Evening all (Labanakt)

Guardian

A man who crept on to the roof of a tanning salon in Wiltshire to spy on a naked woman was caught when the roof collapsed under him.

The Times

Richard Brunstrom, Chief Constable of North Wales, famed for cracking down on errant motorists, revealed in his web journal, how he spent a day off.

While his wife was away, he wrote, he had the opportunity to 'sneak off and have some fun.' He got back into uniform and spent a 12-hour shift on the A497 on the outskirts of Pwllheli along with a camera that 'read 5,891 number plates from which we had 321 hits, resulting in us stopping 109 cars. During the course of the day the team arrested 22 people, mostly for possession of relatively small amounts of cannabis.'

Daily Telegraph

A senior police officer who admitted having sex while on duty was cleared of any offence after he told the court he was always poised and ready to respond to an emergency... because he had his earpiece in.

Daily Mail

A woman from Paisley, near Glasgow, was threatened with an Asbo unless her 13-year-old son stopped practising on his bagpipes at home.

Daily Telegraph

Following claims that police officers were being forced to make ludicrous arrests in an attempt to meet Home Office targets, a Police Dossier of Dubious 'Offences' was produced. It included:

- West Midlands woman arrested on her wedding day for criminal damage to a car park barrier when her foot slipped on the accelerator pedal.
- A child arrested in Kent for throwing a cream bun at a bus.
- Cheshire man cautioned for being 'found in possession of an egg with intent to throw'.
- Kent child who removed a slice of cucumber from a sandwich and threw it at another youngster.
- Two Manchester children arrested under firearms laws for being in possession of a plastic toy pistol.

Daily Mail

Extra police are to be deployed on the streets of Brighton when the moon is full. Neil Rogers, of Deeside, Flintshire, wrote that to counter the effects of a full moon on some of the populace officers should be issued with a garlic flavoured pepper spray and a silver truncheon.

The Times

Two policewomen sped to arrest an attacker in pedal-powered rickshaws. They flagged down two pedicab riders after learning that fellow officers needed help. The pedicab drivers told how they rode them through Hereford rounding corners 'with a motorbike sidecar lean.'

Daily Mirror

The Times' version of the rickshaw raid said that the WPCs 'sat in the back urging their drivers to go faster and encouraged pedestrians and other vehicles to move out of their way by yelling "Nee-naw, nee-naw, nee-naw" at the top of their voices. The rickshaw men said: "We like to think of ourselves as cowboys riding down the bad guys."'

The Times

Martin Hallam, of Oxford, writes about the 1960s when he was a policeman in Winchester. TV personality Hughie Green, of Opportunity Knocks, reported his car had broken down and asked the police to arrange a lift for him to London. A gnarled old policeman advised: 'Go to the bypass, stick up your thumb, and see if opportunity knocks.'

Daily Telegraph

John Chatfield, of Uttoxeter, Staffordshire, saw a report about fake £20 notes being in circulation, along with a quote from a police sergeant: 'About three weeks ago we saw a rise in fake £30 notes, and that is something that is more serious.'

Daily Mail

The *Financial Times* ran a series questioning the behaviour of lawyers:
- Why did the lawyer cross the road? To distribute his calling card to the victims of a five-car pile-up on the other side.
- What do you call 500 lawyers at the bottom of the sea? A good start.
- How many lawyers does it take to change a light bulb? How many can you afford?
- What is the difference between a lawyer and a rat both lying dead on the road? There are skid marks in front of the rat.

Financial Times

In Stroud, Gloucestershire, a man was given an Asbo banning him from yelling abusive and racist comments at his TV.

Sun

A woman who was tied to a refrigerator door at gunpoint by two raiders has been praised for her coolness by Tonbridge police.

Kent and Sussex Courier

David Wills, of Southampton, wrote about solicitors' charges and revealed the following extract from a Bill of Costs raised by his firm in 1907:

> To attending you when asked if we had your mother's will.
> We replied that we would search. 6s 8d
> We searched but did not find it. 6s 8d
> Suggested you should see if the bank had it. 6s 8d
> Letter to the bank asking if it was there. 3s 6d
> Ultimately finding the will in our safe and attending the reading of it. 13s 4d.

Mr Wills ends his letter with: 'We are happy to say that our procedures are considerably more efficient nowadays'.

Daily Telegraph

David Spark, of Great Ayton, Yorkshire, recalls an (apocryphal) solictor's bill:

To crossing the street to say good morning to you. 6s 8d

To crossing back on finding it was not you. 6s 8d

Daily Telegraph

The Rev. W. N. C. Girard, of Balsham, Cambridgeshire wrote to the *Daily Telegraph* about a lawyer's bill sent to the estate of a man whose will he had drawn up. It included the item: 'To attending on you for your signature, but you were dead.'

Daily Telegraph

Police appealed for witnesses after a woman put her toddler into a pushchair on display in a Plymouth store – and walked out with it.

Western Morning News

Clive Anderson, former practising barrister turned successful comedy writer and TV and radio presenter, was rueful about his day job: 'It's just 99% of lawyers who give the rest a bad name.'

Guardian

Retired vicar's wife Ann Laycock, of Ashton-under-Lyne, Greater Manchester, who was shot at by youths in her local park, was advised by police to walk her dog somewhere else in future.

Daily Mail

A gunman attempting to hold up a Tesco petrol station in Cheltenham did not allow for the formidable 51-year-old Linda Faulkner behind the counter. Instead of surrendering the cash from her till she told the raider that she was too busy to deal with him. 'I just got on with it,' she said later. 'British people don't stop work just because someone is trying to bully us with guns.'

Daily Mail

A thief who tried to hand herself in at her local police station in Kent for stealing £3,000 was instructed to go to a police station nine miles away in Canterbury. She was told 'We can't do it today – it's a Bank Holiday. Come back later.'

Sun

In the relentless war on villains, the Serious Organised Crime Agency set up a confidentiality hotline for the public in October 2006. In November 2007 The Times reported 'it is manned five days a week and, thus far, has taken 16 calls. One reported the theft of a bicycle. Another complaint was that someone was smoking in a bank.'

The Times

41

A woman from Aberavon, South Wales, falsely claimed that she was living apart from her husband and fiddled benefits totalling £8,832. She was ordered to pay it back at £10 a month and she will be 109 if she ever gets to make the final payment.

Sun

(This recalls the story of the man in a similar predicament who protested that he was already over 80. 'Just do the best you can', advised the kindly magistrate.)

UKTV Gold invited viewers to nominate the most ridiculous law on English statute books. Strong contenders included:

- Oliver Cromwell's attempt to combat gluttony by banning the eating of mince pies on Christmas Day.
- A 19th century London by-law which allowed pregnant women to relieve themselves in a policeman's helmet.
- The law that will find you guilty of treason if you stick a postage stamp on an envelope with the monarch's head upside-down.

Winner of the contest was the law which bans you from dying in the Houses of Parliament. Anyone who manages to break this law is technically entitled to a state funeral.

Independent

A newly recruited policeman of Swanage, Dorset, recalls walking the beat with an experienced colleague when they came across scrumpers clambering over a wall with their pullovers bulging with stolen apples. His mentor ordered the boys to empty their booty on to the grass, gave each miscreant a sharp slap on the hand with a leather strap, and said: 'Don't let me catch you again.' The scrumpers ran off and the old-fashioned bobby said: 'Stick a few in your pockets – pity we can't take 'em all'.

Daily Mail

A Scotsman convicted of beating up his partner turned out to be an anger management counsellor.

Independent on Sunday

A rape trial was halted after defence counsel accused the judge of falling asleep. Next day Geoffrey W. Davey reminded The Times of an incident in Darlington County Court when the judge closed his eyes. From the back of the court came the comment: 'The old b*****d has gone to sleep'. The judge opened one eye and replied: 'The old b*****d hasn't'.

The Times

A judge ordered a man from Ramsgate, Kent, to pay his former wife £1 for the pineapple he damaged when he hit her with it during an argument.

Thanet Times

Judge Jeremy Roberts adjourned a kidnap case at the Old Bailey and went to watch his horse race at Ascot. It came 12th.

Sunday Telegraph

The Police Federation magazine *Police* tells of thieves who raided a soccer clubhouse in Surrey. They wheeled away their haul of drink on the club's white-line marking machine – and the police tracked down the villains by following the white line.

Daily Mail

Suspicious staff in a Portsmouth store checked on a man when he went into one of their changing rooms. They found he was wearing a bra and knickers he had stolen for his wife.

Sun / Sunday Telegraph

A thief stole a briefcase from a synagogue in Stamford Hill, North London. All it contained was a set of circumcision tools.

Sun

In Scotland, it is illegal to be drunk in charge of a cow.

Observer

A Swindon man who dialled 999 when thieves tried to steal his cannabis plants was arrested when police found 46 plants at his home.

Western Daily Press

When Thames river police cautioned a woman yachtsman for speeding they said: 'Who do you think you are – Tracy Edwards?' 'Yes', replied the lady skippering *Maiden II*, the proven fastest yacht in the world.

The Times

A thief who has been taking furniture piece by piece from a fast food restaurant in Norwich has been invited by the owner to take a sixth chair to complete a dining set.

Norwich Evening News

A thief snatched a handbag from an 86-year-old woman who was out with her dog at Netley Abbey, Southampton – then found the handbag contained only the contents of a poop-scoop.

Daily Telegraph

A burglar who stole a BMW from outside a house he had broken into in Old Basing, Hampshire, was arrested next morning when police found him asleep inside it.

The Times

A thief hiding in bushes after stealing a battery-operated Buzz Lightyear toy from a Hereford shop was caught when police heard the intergalactic law enforcer shouting: 'Buzz Lightyear... permission to engage'.

Daily Telegraph

BARMY BRITAIN

A Mafia hitman charged with two murders told a court: 'It was not me. That night I was killing someone else.'

Independent

CHAPTER 4

BEST OF BRITISHNESS

When an earthquake damaged homes in Kent, victims went down the pub to watch football...

Rowan Atkinson's Mr Bean is a clumsy, gurning, bumbling, birdbrain – and undeniably British...

If you ask a non-Brit to describe Mr Bean, these are the words they deliver back: 'Hapless, awkward, self-conscious, childlike, disaster prone....and British.'

Guardian

Next day *Guardian* reader Brian Denoon, of Inverness wrote: 'Your appreciation of Mr Bean as the epitome of Britishness will boost the desire of Scots to become independent. This cringeworthy creature could not be anything other than English.'

Guardian

There was a very British response when the fourth largest UK earthquake shook Kent in April 2007 – people emerged from their damaged homes and went down the pub to watch football.

Independent on Sunday

British tradesmen drink the equivalent of 1.3 BATHFULS of tea each year.

Direct Line

When packing for their holidays 51% of Britons take baked beans, 46% HP sauce, 23% teabags and 19% loo rolls.

Independent on Sunday

During a 2007 visit to Washington, then Prime Minister Tony Blair demonstrated once again that he is truly a man-of-the-people.

After talking about his plans to promote understanding among people of different faiths and bring peace to the Middle East he went on to tackle a problem which really does concern the British: the difficulty of finding a really good cup of tea. 'This is serious,' he said. 'This is a British tradition that must not be lost. If I were running for office again, I'd make it a major part of any platform.'

Daily Telegraph

Britons have a bewildering lack of knowledge about their country according to a survey commissioned by UKTV History. It revealed:

- Four in ten think the bulldog is the animal that symbolises the country. It is, of course, the lion, which is has been part of the Royal Arms since the Plantagenets.

- A quarter said the Lost Gardens of Heligan in Cornwall are among the Seven Wonders of the World, confusing them with the Hanging Gardens of Babylon.

- One in five think the Pennines are between France and Spain.

- Fifteen per cent think Hadrian's Wall is in China.

The Times

The 2007 Rough Guide names 25 things to do in Britain before you die. Among them:

- See the Belfast murals.
- Sup Guinness.
- Breathe in the sea air in Tobermory.
- Hunt ghosts in York.
- Gorge your way through Birmingham's Balti triangle.
- Go clubbing in London.
- Visit the best beach in Britain: Holkham, Norfolk. (The Queen's bathing hut is in the woods just behind the nudist beach.)

Daily Telegraph

Journalist Cole Moreton went in search of polite society after it was reported that schools were to have Civility Classes. When a man dropped his plastic pint beer glass in a pub Moreton said: 'Excuse me, I think you've dropped something.' The beery bloke lurched forward, chest thrust out and fists clenched, slurring: 'Wassyer problem?'

Maybe, wrote Moreton, if the man had been to a civility class, he would have said: 'Yes, I see the error of my ways. I will hasten to a bin. Thank you for helping me to be a better citizen.' Or maybe not.

Modern Britons are rude and getting ruder.

Independent on Sunday

Bestselling American author Bill Bryson has a deep knowledge and an absolute passion for England's heritage. So it was no surprise when, in May 2007, he became president of the Campaign for the Protection of Rural England. He lived in England for a long time and then went back to the States, intending his return to be permanent. But, he says, he 'spent the next eight years pining for Radio 4, the English sense of humour – and Branston pickle.'

He once wrote of Blackpool: 'On Friday and Saturday nights it has more public toilets than anywhere else. Elsewhere they call them doorways.'

And of Liverpool: 'They were having a festival of litter when I arrived.'

Guardian

In February 2008 a small addition was made to England's treasury of listed buildings – a rare surviving example of a late 18th century privy, even rarer because it is a three-seater where parents and child 'could sit down peacefully together and let nature take its course'. It is in the grounds of an old farmhouse in Kent and the proud owner says: 'It faces towards the evening sun and is the most delightful place to sit with a glass of wine and the door open, and just be peaceful and sit and think'.

Guardian

The report of the three-seat privy reminded David Critchlow, of Poole, Dorset, of the time he stopped at a cottage in Cornwall so that a friend could relieve herself. The elderly woman owner told her where the privy was and said: 'Do mind out for the chicken'. When the friend opened the door the chicken was nesting on the second hole.

Guardian

Only a third of Britons would mind missing the Queen's Christmas speech. 62% would not mind if the Trooping of the Colour disappeared.

But fewer than a third would give up Sunday lunch or beer in pints, and 85% would not surrender days out at the seaside.

YouGov survey in the *Daily Mail*

'This country is a blessed nation. The British are special, the world knows it. This is the greatest nation on Earth.' (Tony Blair's exit speech, 10 May 2007.) Next day the Guardian asked: 'Are we the greatest?', and listed some areas where we excel:

- 38.1% of British 15-year-olds have had sex – the highest figure in the developed world.
- British house price inflation is higher than any other developed nation.
- Haydn Pitchforth, of Leeds, is world champion bog snorkeller.

Guardian

How could Hitler ever have made the mistake of thinking that he could conquer this blessed nation? On 14 May 1940 the *Manchester Guardian* (as it then was) reported Churchill's 'I have nothing to offer but blood, toil, tears and sweat' speech.

It also carried an article that dealt with another pressing matter indicating the gravity of the sacrifices facing a nation in peril. People, it said, can affect an economy by doing without a maid – making her services available for more essential work.

Guardian

And Kaiser Wilhelm was surely foolish to ignore this admonition: 'We give this solemn warning to the Kaiser: The *Skibereen Eagle* has its eye on you'.

The *Skibereen Eagle* quoted in *The Times*

A *Daily Telegraph* reader was invited to a wedding in Salzburg which required guests to turn up in national costume. He asked for advice and got this from Richard Woodward of Nottingham:

- Develop an enormous beer gut and a bright pink suntan.
- Wear a beer stained England football shirt.
- Behave boorishly.
- Chant futile songs and demand to know where the nearest kebab shop is.

Alan Wright, of Bristol, said that the choice of national costume should comprise knotted handkerchief, white shirt with rolled up sleeves, grey flannels supported by braces, and sandals with socks.

Daily Telegraph

A survey reveals that Britons have collectively wasted £169 billion buying things they never wear or hardly ever use. The average person has squandered £3,685 on pointless purchases. Half admit to having expensive clothing they never wear, 35% have a pair of unworn shoes, and 35% are members of a gym they never attend.

Daily Telegraph

The British take their traditions seriously – and dangerously. The annual cheese rolling tradition takes place on Cooper's Hill, near Stroud, which has, in places, a one-in-three gradient. Participants hurl themselves after huge, wheel-shaped Double Gloucester Cheeses, and spectators gasp at the speed of the races and the violence of the tumbles. The cheeses sometimes veer into the crowd as they hurtle down the steep hill.

The *Times* headline on the 2007 event was:

CHEESE ROLLERS GET OFF LIGHTLY. ONLY 20 HURT

The organiser commented: 'Last year it was almost double that. Some would like to see it stopped, but it's a British tradition.'

The Times

The British builder's mug of tea is as much a part of his tools of the trade as his shovel or electric drill. Tony Aldous, of London, told the Guardian of the days when he worked on a building site:

'A galvanised bucket of dubious cleanliness was half filled from a hosepipe and a packet of tea, half a packet of sugar and a tin of condensed milk was added and then brought to the boil. 'A matter of taste,' said Mr Aldous, 'but it certainly laid the dust'.

Guardian

Great Britain, once epitomised by the stiff upper lip, modesty and minding your own business, has been replaced by a land of burger-eating binge drinkers, pornography addicts and followers of so-called celebrities. The 2007 *Lonely Planet* guide says:

- More Britons vote in TV talent shows than in elections.
- Sherwood Forest now has more tourists than trees.
- Rudeness and lack of generosity tarnish Britons.
- They have a poor dress sense and are noisy, untidy and are miserly tippers.
- Without doubt you can find great food in Britain... It's just that not all Brits seem to like eating it.

The Times

Britons have voted Stonehenge the most disappointing tourist spectacle in the UK. Also on the list are:
- Blackpool Tower
- Land's End
- Diana's Memorial Fountain
- The London Eye
- Buckingham Palace
- White Cliffs of Dover
- Big Ben

The problem might be that people come to the most well known sights with expectations already raised too high – and an unrealistic desire to see them minus the crowds.

Guardian

In August 2007 Southwold on the Sussex coast was named in a survey as the quintessential British holiday resort. The survey looked at factors that people thought made resorts uniquely British and Southwold topped the poll because of its traditional beach huts, its large choice of fish and chip shops, a working lighthouse, donkey rides, plenty of deckchairs, amusement arcades, scenic countryside – and rude postcards.

The availability of fish and chips was considered the most important factor.

Daily Telegraph

David Joss Buckley, of London, didn't think much of August 2007, and wrote to the Guardian:

'South London, August 21. First hot-water bottle of the year. Is this a record?'

Guardian

Ralph Hawkins, of Ware, Hertfordshire, wrote how he met tea made by the method described by Mr Aldous when on his first guard duty on national service. Kept hot on the stove all night it became the colour of dark mahogany 'with a taste all its own'. The guard commander called it 'desert tea – without the sand'.

Guardian

August 2007 was a wicked month. Wet, cold, windy. 80 coaches brought 5,000 French people to Margate, Kent, for 'a taste of the real England'. They were greeted by 'gunmetal skies, horizontal winds and a blattering drizzle to sample the traditional British seaside pursuits of huddling in bus shelters and picking sand from their sandwiches.'

The *Guardian* printed a picture of French visitors sitting on towels on the damp sand underneath a sign which said: 'Welcome to Margate's Main Sands. Deckchairs and Sunbeds for your Pleasure and Leisure'.

Roger Latchford, deputy leader of the local council, said: 'I did a sun dance with our events team. Regrettably it doesn't seem to have worked.'

Guardian

The *Daily Telegraph* gathered together some definitions of a British gentleman:

- A man who still uses the butter knife even when dining alone.
- A man who has never previously heard your joke.
- A man who believes a woman when he knows she is telling lies.
- A man who can play the bagpipes but doesn't.

Daily Telegraph

Following stories that more and more Brits are leaving to live abroad, the *Daily Telegraph* published Thirty Reasons to Stay in Britain. Reason number one was that there is never a problem getting a Polish plumber, followed by:

- You can't get a decent chicken tikka masala anywhere else.
- A day at Lord's, the most civilised sporting venue in the world.
- Cheese rolling in Gloucestershire. Bog snorkelling in Wales. Barrel burning in Lewes. No one does bonkers traditions like they do here.
- Best place for barbecuing in the rain.

Daily Telegraph

The British do not like folk messing about with their beloved icons. Hence all the hoo-ha when marmalade-loving Paddington Bear was depicted enjoying Marmite sandwiches.

'What next?' wrote Keith Whitford, of Cornwall, 'Desperate Dan tucking into spinach and ricotta pie?'

'Whatever next?' wrote Colin Bath, of Somerset. 'Pooh and peanut butter?'

The Times

To see Paddington eating a Marmite sandwich somehow undermines the marrow of our being.

It is like seeing Winston Churchill lighting up a pipe.

Independent on Sunday

Elaine Davies, of Somerset, wrote: 'The furore could have been avoided if the advertiser had depicted Paddington enjoying my favourite: Marmite and marmalade sandwiches.'

The Times

What a splendid lot of old-fashioned traditionalists the British are. A report which looked at the changing face of UK society showed people yearning for the return of:
- Rag and bone men
- Bus conductors
- Bobbies on the beat
- District nurses

Many would like to see the back of:
- Congestion zones
- Speed cameras
- Outdoor smoking areas
- Bus lanes
- Outdoor urinals
- Smelly hot dog vendors

In a report called *Local Life* by the Somerfield supermarket chain there were also some who favoured the return of the stocks, witches stakes and heads on spikes.

Daily Telegraph

When a newspaper invited readers to submit new designs for the backs of British coins, one reader suggested: 'A couple of yobs dancing on a car bonnet or a trio of legless ladettes in the gutter.'

Daily Telegraph

The *Daily Telegraph* reported that Havant Borough Council in Hampshire was 'facing rebellion' after switching the brand of tea it serves. One member said: 'I do not think it should be forced upon us. We are British after all.'

Daily Telegraph

In 2007 Prime Minister Gordon Brown had 'a simple wheeze' – a motto to capture what makes Britain great. Early efforts collected by *The Times* included:

- Britain – a terribly nice place
- Stubborn to the point of greatness
- Less stuffy than we sound
- Turned out nice again
- Sorry, is this the queue?
- Dipso fatso bingo asbo Tesco
- At least we're not French

The Times

Peter Long, of Southampton, thought the motto capturing the spirit of our modern nation is: 'What's in it for me?'

The Times

The winning entry in a survey to find a 'national motto':

No Motto Please, We Are British.

The Week magazine

Cerne Abbas (population 800), a Dorset community watched over by a 180ft chalk figure of a naked giant, has been identified as Britain's most desirable village. Despite its small size it has two tea rooms, a Post Office, a primary school, a new village hall, sports fields, a doctor's surgery, a 14th century church – and three pubs.

The Times

When Roger Cooper was released from an Iranian prison after serving more than five years he said: 'Anyone who has attended an English public school and served in the British Army is quite well prepared for a spell in a Third World prison'.

David Staples, London N8.

The Times

Madonna says she is delighted to be living in Britain – partly because Britons '...are not as rude and obnoxious as Americans'. She also thinks English swear words are 'more charming and more colourful.'

Daily Mail

The English section of the guests' information notice in a third floor hotel room in Copenhagen read: 'In the event of fire, open a window and announce your presence in a seemly manner.'
R. A. Morley, Southport.

The Times

The British, who like to believe that the Germans have no sense of humour, found it difficult to swallow the crack made by Tilman Hanckel, the new cultural attaché at the German Embassy in London. Hanckel told a BBC interviewer: 'I came to London in July. In a way, it's my first Third World posting'.

Daily Mail

The *Daily Mail* accompanied its report on this story with three anti-German jokes and three anti-English jokes – including these two.

• Why did the sun never set on the British empire? Because God would never trust an Englishman in the dark.
• What's the difference between a German and a shopping trolley? A shopping trolley has a mind of its own.

Daily Mail

Rude, narrow minded, not very sexy and the food is rubbish. Meet the British as seen through a Reader's Digest poll in 19 European countries. But at least they thought that we had the best sense of humour.

The Times

Arrogant, rain sodden, narrow-minded, old-fashioned, white-skinned pacifist toffs. Meet the British as seen through the eyes of American teenagers surveyed by the British council.

But most of the students polled could not name the four components of the United Kingdom and one said: 'I don't think they kill each other as much as we do.'

The Times

The Europeans polled by the *Digest* also thought that Britain had contributed more to the world than anyone else – 'although this seems based on our invention of football, not our great feats of discovery, adventure and exploration'.

The Times

The shipping forecast, broadcast four times a day by the BBC, has become cult listening, much loved by thousands of listeners who have never boarded a ship. The forecast is an eccentric list of winds in sea areas around Britain and has become like a familiar poem that defines British cultural heritage. It has inspired poetry, literature, works of art and tea towels. So there is much anguish that the name of one of the sea areas is to be changed from Finisterre to Fitzroy. It brings no comfort that the name Fitzroy has been chosen in memory of the founding father of the Met Office, Admiral Robert Fitzroy, who allegedly committed suicide in 1865 after forecasting the weather wrong.

Guardian

Foreigners often mock the British for the way in which we go on about the weather. What they fail to realise is that our weather is just a damn sight more interesting than anybody else's. Foreign weather is so utterly predictable that it is simply not worth talking about. Where else but in Britain can one wake up on July morning not knowing whether to put on a sweater and sou'wester or a T-shirt and shorts.

Daily Telegraph

The English are completely mad with their pets. It's not unusual for police forces to be mobilised to save a cat or dog from drowning.

French writer Agnes Catherine Poirer in her book *Les Nouveaux Anglais*

Daily Mail

Next day the *Daily Telegraph* reported that fireman Doug Little saved a hamster with the kiss of life in a smoke-filled flat in Portsmouth.

Daily Telegraph

Agnes Poirer's book also suggests that British society – including the upper class – is almost entirely reliant on alcohol and complains that in too many pubs the food comes straight from the microwave after days in the freezer. 'Unremarkable wines are the norm.'

But, without doubt, the British are still the funniest, particularly about sex, which is complicated, clumsy and tortuous.

Daily Mail

The *Guardian*'s coverage of the Poirer book quotes her on the British being the kings of eccentricity: devotees of the queue, ardent monarchists, fanatical darts players, weather obsessives, and eaters of toast with baked beans in tomato sauce.'

The British Library's acoustics are perfect. When one eminent reader broke wind there the cacophony ricocheted around the building with appalling ferocity, like a sniper's bullet. Being terribly British, no-one said a thing.

Observer

'It's amazing – while 94 per cent of the British public insist they don't use cannabis a third of us know someone who does'.

News of the World

Many Britons remain reluctant to give up their yards and inches to comply with EU instructions to go metric. Graham A. Feakins of London SE24 was delighted to report that 'on a road sign near me there is a low bridge said to be 3.5 metres high, 70 yards ahead.'

Independent

'We are still the second most important country on Earth. The trick of maintaining such influence, of course, is to go around pretending to be very bumbling and hopeless and self-deprecating, a skill at which we excel.'

Boris Johnson, who was elected as Mayor of London in May 2008.

Daily Telegraph

CHAPTER 5
MEDIA MADNESS

Astrological magazine to close publication 'due to unforeseen circumstances'...

Duncan Campbell's Diary in the *Guardian* picked up on a Sun story about a man who wanted to be a woman – and cut off his testicles.

BUILDER CHOPS NUTS AND BOLTS was the headline, and this reminded Campbell of a policeman who did the same and carried on being a copper. His headline was NO NOBBY BOBBY KEEPS HIS JOBBY.

Guardian

MAN WITH FALSE LEG HIT WITH TOILET LID
Watford Observer headline which was a strong contender for Headline of the Week in the *Guardian* Diary on August 30 2007.

The case of a man who mistakenly used a tube of super glue instead of haemorrhoid cream was raised in a Commons committee as an example of unacceptable press intrusion after a tabloid newspaper ran the story under the headline:

JOHN'S GONE POTTY AND GLUED UP HIS BOTTY

Daily Telegraph

The Press Association reports that a woman who was found headless in a laundry bag had died from neck injuries caused by a sharp instrument.

Guardian

Headline on a story about the 1957 Trans-Antarctic expedition:

VIVIAN FUCHS OFF TO THE ANTARTIC
Ken Battersby, Millom, Cumbria.

Daily Telegraph

The World Association of Newspapers ran full-page ads in May 2007 under the headline: PEOPLE SAY THE SILLIEST THINGS. It included:

- **Smoking kills. 'If you are killed you've lost a very important part of your life.' (Brooke Shields)**
- **'When your back's against the wall it's time to turn around and fight' (John Major)**

All papers

The *Guardian* Diary's Headline of the Week competition produced this strong contender from the Stranraer and Wigtownshire Gazette:

MAN WHO KILLED BEST FRIEND WARNED TO BEHAVE

Guardian

It was followed by 'a first class effort' from the *Star of Malaysia*:

STUDENT MAY BE SUSPENDED FOR STRANGLING HIS TEACHER

Guardian

Rupert Murdoch became concerned about the size of the drinks served up by the *Sun*'s first editor, Larry Lamb. He complained: 'I don't mind them drinking my Scotch, but do they have to drink it out of goldfish bowls?'

Sun

Former *Daily Express* editor Derek Marks once tried to phone the editor of the paper's William Hickey gossip column at four in the afternoon. When he was told that the editor was still at lunch he demanded to know when he went to lunch. He was told, perfectly truthfully: 'Yesterday, sir'.

Sun

A policeman told an Old Bailey jury that when he saw a man holding up a *Guardian* very close to his face he thought it was 'rather strange behaviour'. Judge Martin Stephens, QC, interjected: 'Reading the *Guardian*, you mean?'

Guardian

'The old pouffe blamed for the fire at Douglas Cottages, as reported last week, referred to an item of furniture and not the owner'.

Dunoon Observer

Some recent headlines:
- POLICE BEGIN CAMPAIGN TO RUN DOWN JAYWALKERS
- MINERS REFUSE TO WORK AFTER DEATH
- SCHOOLS DROP-OUTS CUT IN HALF
- RED TAPE HOLDS UP NEW BRIDGE

Timothy Haas, *Reader's Digest*

Peter Ackroyd was 23 when he walked into the office of the *Spectator* magazine in 1973 to ask if he might do a review. The then editor, George Gale, asked if there was anything which might affect Ackroyd's suitability. 'A bit of a drinking problem,' said Ackroyd. He was hired on the spot as literary editor.

Daily Telegraph

There are many jokes about how mean the BBC can be. A Times reader recalled how a learned professor, on being told that his talk had been accepted for a fee of £25, was said to have replied thanking the BBC with words to the effect: 'I enclose a cheque for £25.'

David Townley, Banstead, Surrey. *The Times*

The true inspiration for the BBC's Flowerpot Men has been a source of dispute for years. The main cause of controversy is the word 'flobbadob'. One of the men involved in the dispute claims that the word was invented by him and his brother to describe the sound they made when breaking wind in the bath.

Independent on Sunday

The *Astrological Magazine* announces that it is to cease publication 'due to unforeseen circumstances'.

The Times

A *Brighton Argus* reader sent the paper a photograph of an exquisite rainbow over the seafront. They printed it in black and white.

Guardian

K. B. Thomas, of Shepperton, Middlesex, writes of a Northern Nigerian tribal chief being apprehended for eating the local tax inspector. 'How much duller life will be when one can no longer alight upon such a sentence in the *Daily Telegraph*'s inimitable Obituaries page.'

Daily Telegraph

Andrew Pierce tells of meeting the Queen at a St James's Palace reception. To my astonishment, she paused in front of me, said hello, and asked what I did. I stammered and muttered something like 'You can't speak to me'.

Unruffled, she said: 'But I can... so who are you?'

'I'm a journalist and was told that the Queen never speaks to the press.'

'Who do you work for?'

'*The Times*.'

'Ah. Rupert Murdoch. You're quite right. I can't talk to you.'

Daily Telegraph

CHAPTER 6
ROYAL FLUSH

**It's an honour to be insulted
by Royalty...**

A government minister was attending an audience with the Queen when her mobile phone rang and she quickly rejected the call. 'I hope that wasn't anyone too important,' said Her Majesty.

The Times

Humorist Alan Coren died in October 2007 and the *Independent*'s obituary recalled an item on The News Quiz about Princess Diana and her campaign against landmines. 'I don't know much about Diana or about landmines' said Alan, 'but I do know that you poke either at your peril.' An item which was deleted by the dear old BBC when the programme was repeated.

Independent

Ian Botham chatted with the Queen while receiving his knighthood and Kelvin Mackenzie wondered if he told her about the last ball he bowled in cricket – to Australia's legendary David Boon. As he ran up Botham unzipped his flies, produced the family jewels and then bowled.

Sun

The Duke of Edinburgh met a group of belly dancers in Swansea and said: 'I thought Eastern women just sat around smoking pipes and eating sweets all day.'

His outburst stunned the dancers, but one of them said: 'He is very down-to-earth – but, to be honest, it's an honour to be insulted by Royalty. Anyway, when you're a belly dancer you've heard it all before.'

Daily Telegraph

'Bloody hell, Ma'am. He oughtn't to be in there!' Buckingham Palace maid on seeing intruder Michael Fagan sitting on the Queen's bed in 1982.

Mail on Sunday

Police discovered an intruder in the grounds of Buckingham Palace. He said he was looking for Princess Anne and was taken to a mental hospital.

The Times

Billy Tallon, who died aged 71 in November 2007, was the Queen Mother's favourite page. Always known as Backstairs Billy, he spent 51 years in Royal service. He was instantly recognisable on public occasions, such as the Queen Mother's 100th birthday pageant, when he led his royal mistress's corgis (Minnie and Rush) onto Horse Guards Parade, grandly pausing to chat with the crowd as if to the manner born. The story goes that on one occasion she heard him gossiping with another male servant and called out: 'When you old queens have finished this old Queen would like a gin and tonic.'

Daily Mail

Billy's lethal mixture was nine-tenths gin and one-tenth tonic. He was always there to console her whenever she backed a losing horse – which was more often than she cared to admit.

Daily Mail

'One of my worst moments was when I drank from my finger dipping bowl at a royal party. Not only did I drink it, I also asked for the recipe.'

Tara Palmer-Tomkinson quoted in the *Sunday Times*.

When Prince William and his girlfriend Kate Middleton split up there were unconfirmed reports that palace circles did not like the way her mother chewed gum and called the lavatory a toilet. Newspapers rushed to remind us that Britain is still a class minefield and Les Hearn, of London, wrote to the Guardian saying: 'We call it "The Throne". Would that be posh enough?'

Guardian

Some were also sniffy about Kate's mother saying 'Pleased to meet you' to the Queen.

Maggie Hughes, of Gnosall, Staffordshire, wrote about a terrifying old lady who, when introduced to someone who said 'Pleased to meet you', replied: 'Do you always leap to such sudden conclusions'.

Daily Telegraph

Sixty years ago there was controversy over souvenirs deemed unsuitable as tributes to the Royal Family.

The item which most got up the noses of Palace officials was a handkerchief featuring portraits of the future Queen and the Duke of Edinburgh. One government official suggested that the handkerchiefs might be acceptable – provided that people did not actually blow their noses on the royal portraits.

Daily Mail

The *Sun* splashed, as a ROYAL EXCLUSIVE, that the Queen is a Gooner (that's an Arsenal supporter) just like her mother was.

The Page One story was illustrated with a mock-up picture of Queen Elizabeth II wearing a bejewelled tiara – and an Arsenal scarf.

On Page 8, under the headline GUNN EII RS, there is another mock-up showing the Monarch wearing an elegant pastel blue evening gown with matching handbag – and an Arsenal shirt bearing a Fly Emirates ad.

The ever-present, but never identified, senior royal source is quoted: 'Her Majesty has been fond of Arsenal for over 50 years. Her late mother was a self-confessed Gooner, due largely to her admiration of their former player Dennis Compton.'

Sun

Reaction was swift after Prince Charles, visiting Abu Dhabi, asked if they had tried getting McDonald's banned.

Along with their coverage of his remark, newspapers ran a story saying that his Duchy Originals Organic Beef Cornish Pasty has 132 more calories than a Big Mac and is higher in salt and saturated fat.

Daily Telegraph

'Don't buy a new hat, don't mimic her accent, and don't call her Liz'. Advice given to Americans in advance of the Queen's 2007 visit to the USA.

A hotline gives tips on royal etiquette and says one should not curtsy or bow ('Bowing is not required of U.S. citizens').

If the Queen offers her hand one should take it gently and address her as Your Majesty or Ma'am (which rhymes with jam).

Daily Mail

When Queen Elizabeth II visited the White House in May 2007, President George Bush made a welcome speech, saying: 'You helped our nation celebrate its bicentennial in 17... in... 1976'. He then made light of his slip by shooting a quick look at the Queen and saying: 'You gave me a look that only a mother could give a child.'

Guardian and every other paper in the land

Perhaps a bigger gaffe was made when the Prince of Wales visited Ronald Reagan at the White House in 1981. The president recorded in his diary that 'horror of horrors' Charles was served tea with the tea bag still in it.

The Times

The Duke of Edinburgh discussed space walks with British-born astronaut Piers Sellers and asked: 'What do you do about bodily functions?'

Sellers replied: 'You can last up to ten hours. When you get back inside someone helps you off with your space suit – then it's a rush.'

Times writer Alan Hamilton commented: 'A bit like a long day of royal engagements, really.'

The Times

Courtiers tried to block the sale of 'tasteless' memorabilia surrounding the wedding of the Queen and the Duke of Edinburgh in November 1947.

The Cheadle Fabric Company caused concern with its handkerchiefs featuring the couple's portraits. The Home Office suggested they would be acceptable provided people did not actually blow their noses on the royal portraits.

Daily Telegraph

'If you travel as much as we do, you appreciate how much more comfortable aircraft have become. Unless you travel in something called economy class, which sounds ghastly.'

Duke of Edinburgh quoted in the *Observer*

In her 50+ years on the throne the Queen has received 1,500 state gifts – including a samovar from Boris Yeltsin and a computer from Ronald Reagan. She has often received live presents, including armadillos, anteaters, jaguars, beavers, turtles, an elephant and a canary.

Independent

The Queen has never been known for sentimentality and does not believe in having a memorial to the late Queen Mother. But each of her corgis, dachshunds and labradors that have died has a miniature tombstone in the grounds of Sandringham.

The Times

The Queen's chef discloses that Her Majesty insists on cucumber sandwiches being cut octagonally. The corgis are fed on boiled cabbage, long grain rice and lamb's kidneys.

Sunday Times

I have managed to recreate Prince Harry's hairstyle by cycling for five hours on a windy day.

Michael Hall, Bury St. Edmonds.
Daily Telegraph

The Queen once gave all the staff at Sandringham a potted chrysanthemum for Christmas. The gifts were all accompanied with a little handwritten note saying 'When the plant dies, please return the pot to the head gardener'.

Observer

The Queen's grandmother, Queen Mary, used to amuse friends by throwing pieces of cake in the air and catching them in her mouth.

Daily Mail

After listening to a list of his achievements on receiving an honorary doctorate, the Duke of Edinburgh said: 'I was wondering who the hell he was talking about.'

Sunday Times

In the presence of Her Majesty nobody behaves naturally. The moment a royal visit is over, the relief is intense. 'When royalty leaves the room,' said Joyce Grenfell's mother, 'it's like getting a seed out of your tooth.'

Sunday Telegraph

It seems that when the gaffe-prone Duke of Edinburgh peruses the newspapers – as he does every morning at breakfast – he exclaims ruefully: 'Let's see what I did wrong yesterday.'

Reader's Digest

The Duke makes jokes out of his gaffes, for which he has coined a word: 'Dontopedalogy – the art of opening your mouth and putting your foot in it'

Independent

Princess Diana once told a friend: 'I've told Charles never to wear hats. With his ears, they make him like a Volkswagen Beetle with the doors open'.

Observer

Prince Charles and Camilla were among a group who went for a late swim when there was a swirling mist. The mist suddenly cleared to reveal about 20 nudists on the shore. Nobody was particularly fazed, but it was sweet to see one of the nude ladies trying to curtsy.

Sun

When the Queen visited the Milk Marketing Board's artificial insemination unit she pointed to a specimen and asked: 'What's that?'

'It's a cow's vagina, ma'am'.

Her Majesty didn't blink but just said: 'Ask a silly question...'

Observer

Queen Elizabeth II, one of the richest people in the world, never carries money on her person – but it would be easy for her to lay her hands on some. Her bank, Coutts, has installed a cashpoint inside Buckingham Palace. The machine now represents one quarter of the bank's entire cashpoint network – one of the other three being at Eton College not far from the Queen's other home at Windsor Castle.

Daily Telegraph

Sir Robert Baden-Powell, founder of the Scouts, was the first man to enter Buckingham Palace in shorts.

He wrote asking for permission to do so, thus causing a revolution in court etiquette when the Royal Family were forced to see knees for the first time.

Sandi Toksvig in *Seven* magazine

An MP met the Queen and remarked on the strain it must be having to meet so many strangers. 'It's not as difficult as it might seem,' she replied. 'You see, I don't have to introduce myself. They all seem to know who I am.'

The Times

Prince William and Kate Middleton checked into a resort hotel as Martin and Rosemary. Prince Charles and Camilla once checked in as Fred and Gladys.

Sun

The *Sunday Times* reports: Well might Prince Charles have snapped at Diana (after a row about his relationship with Camilla): 'Do you seriously expect me to be the first Prince of Wales in history not to have a mistress?'

Sunday Times

Is Prince Charles fit to be king? Of course he isn't, wrote Simon Hoggart in the *Guardian*. 'Which of his male ancestors were?'
- George VI hated the job.
- Edward VIII? No way.
- George V – a martinet who loved stamps and killing wildlife.
- Edward II? I think not.

Among the few good monarchs count Victoria and the two Elizabeths. The men have been hopeless.

Guardian

Want to join Prince William's set, described in the *Tatler* as 'the jolliest court in history?' You need to be loyal, vote Conservative, be a good horseman or woman but a terrible dancer, be anti-drugs, have a strong drinking constitution and be 'a good egg'.

Daily Telegraph

How on earth do you find a wedding present for the girl who is to become the Queen of England? Gandhi didn't have a problem: 'I have given all my possessions away', he explained.

Sunday Telegraph

The two royal kneelers used during the wedding service were made from orange boxes due to wartime austerity. Gifts from the public included a hand-knitted cardigan, two pairs of bed socks and a hand-knitted tea cosy.

Sunday Telegraph

When the newly-weds left Buckingham Palace after the wedding breakfast Elizabeth hid her favourite corgi (Susan) under a rug in their carriage so that the dog could go with them.

Sunday Telegraph

When Elizabeth became Queen, Philip knew that he would have to keep one step behind her in public. But when the door is closed on the outside world he is very much the head of the family. There was an occasion at Sandringham when he was driving with the Queen in the passenger seat and an aide in the back. He was driving fast and the Queen asked him to slow down. Philip said: 'One more peep out of you and you can walk the rest of the way.'

Daily Mail

Gyles Brandreth, author of *Philip and Elizabeth: Portrait of a Marriage*, says. She wears the crown, but he wears the trousers.

Sunday Telegraph

Tracy Borman is writing a biography of Henrietta Howard, a cultured woman of the 18th century, who for 20 years was the mistress of George II. The king actually preferred his wife, with whom he was in love, but duty was stern in those days and a monarch had to have a mistress. For all those years, seven days a week, he spent four hours alone with her (from 9pm). No doubt, at first, they did the obvious but eventually they seem to have just talked. One courtier said it worked because he was boring and she was deaf.

Simon Hoggart, *Guardian*

Keeping the monarchy costs every man, woman and child in Britain the equivalent of one loaf of bread a year.

The Times

The Queen's sharp eye for economy is well known in royal circles. Two footmen who were found together in a bath in the Royal Mews explained that they were helping Her Majesty's drive to reduce gas bills.

Observer

To celebrate Queen Elizabeth II making history when, at 81 years and 243 days old, she became the oldest Monarch to sit on the English throne, *The Times* published 81 Facts About the Monarchy, including:

- Queen Elizabeth I owned the world's first flushing toilet, presented to her by her godson, the inventor Sir John Harrington.
- Charles II (The Merry Monarch) fathered 13 children by his mistresses and none by his wife.
- George I and his mistress were known as the Elephant and Castle, because she was so tall and he was so fat.
- Queen Elizabeth II is the only British monarch to have been properly trained to change a spark plug.
- She demoted a footman for feeding her corgis whisky.

The Times

It is said that Prince Charles once chided Ronnie Scott, the jazz club man, for not paying his musicians enough. Ronnie asked the prince what made him think that. 'Because they're all smoking the same cigarette,' replied Charles.

Daily Mail

CHAPTER 7

RUDE BRITANNIA

**'I've lost my phone number.
Can I have yours?'**

The Icelandic Phallological Museum – believed to be the only museum of penises – has 245 examples from animals such as hamsters, horses and whales. It is looking for a human specimen, and diarist Jon Henley said it sounded like a eunuch opportunity.

Guardian

Changing Times:
- 1950 – Average age for a woman to lose virginity is 21. For men it is 20.
- 1960 – Average age for women to lose virginity is down to 19. For men it is 18.
- 2000 – Average person loses virginity at 16. One in five men and one in six women in the 16–24 age range have had more than ten partners.

Guardian

The *Proceedings of the Royal Society* journal says men take the same pleasure out of looking at an attractive female as they do from having a curry.

Daily Telegraph

A couple mounted the stairs to the roof of a London theatre and then mounted each other – not knowing they were in full view of some Soho offices. Workers there filmed the encounter and shared it with the world on YouTube. Hundreds of thousands tuned in to the al fresco romp.

Independent on Sunday

A Durex survey revealed that Britons have sex an average 92 times a year. Greeks score 164, Brazilians 145, Russians and Poles 143.

The survey also said that most Britons are unhappy with their sex lives, but not as unhappy as the Japanese, who scored only 48 times a year.

Sun

Sir Ian McKellen got his kit off when playing King Lear and an anonymous theatregoer emailed Jon Henley's diary: 'Sir Ian is an actor with a large part.'

Guardian

Dan Jones, a painter and writer with a deep interest in the folklore of the playground, has gathered some 400 songs, mainly from schools in his own borough of Tower Hamlets in London's East End. One of them has the catchy lyric:

Ooh, ah, I lost my bra
I left my knickers in my boyfriend's car.

Guardian

Among chat up lines paraded in the *Independent on Sunday*:
- Excuse me, I've lost my phone number. Can I have yours?
- Do you believe in love at first sight or am I going to have to walk past you again?
- I was just wondering if you had any space in your handbag for my Ferrari keys.
- Your eyes are blue like the ocean and baby I'm lost at sea. (This one got the response: 'You must be pissed, luv. My eyes are brown'.)

Independent on Sunday

A Dutchman was caught having sex with a sheep – but the case was thrown out of court because under Dutch law bestiality is not a crime unless it can be proved that the animal did not want to have sex.

Independent on Sunday

Ursula Andress's emergence from the Caribbean in the 1962 James Bond film *Dr No* has been voted the best bikini scene ever. It was followed by a Morecambe and Wise skit which had a half-naked goddess emerging from the ocean inquiring seductively if there was anything they had been missing.

One of the funny men replied: 'You haven't got a chip pan?'

Daily Mail

The late George Melly, musician and author, was also an angler and tells the story of a Scotsman who was a virgin: 'I've never been with a woman, but from what I hear it's not unlike landing a salmon'.

The Times

A man has been placed on the sex offenders' register for pleasuring himself with a bicycle. *The Observer* reported that the BBC News website used a photograph of a bicycle, but 'one can only trust it is not the actual bicycle, as it is an offence to show victims of sex crimes.'

Observer

'I don't know if it is the same with you, Harold, but I find if I don't have sex at least once every 24 hours, I get these goddamn headaches.' The Sunday Times records this 'hitherto unreported comment by President Kennedy to a speechless Harold Macmillan'.

Sunday Times

The *Kama Sutra* was first published in English in 1883, though it remained illegal until 1963. It would take the average couple three and a half years to try every one of the 529 positions described in the book.

Observer

The British Museum's Secretum is a collection of Victorian erotica kept behind locked doors. It represents a magnificent obsession with male genitalia. About 30 people a year apply for permission to view. The majority are women.

Daily Mail

John Mortimer remembers 'a terrible moment in my life when, at lunch with a girlfriend and her mother, I misjudged the legs under the table and started to caress the mother'.

Daily Mail

Retired agony aunt Claire Rayner says a memorable problem letter she received read: 'My husband won't make love to me in any way, even a kiss or a cuddle. His father's the same'.

Daily Mail

CHAPTER 8
POLITICS

**Harold Wilson liked to say of Tony Benn:
'He immatures with age'...**

Prime Minister Gordon Brown lost an eye as a 16-year-old rugby player and a rude MP told him: 'I can always tell which is your false eye. It's the one with warmth in it.'

Sun

Julian Glover's review of Alistair Campbell's diary says that the 750-page book 'can be boiled down to a single sentence: "How me and Tony stuffed the media and changed the world"'.

Guardian

In the week when the Scottish National Party did rather well in the May 2007 elections Andrew Gimson of the *Daily Telegraph* produced a quote from a Scottish voter on SNP leader Alex Salmond: 'That man is so pleased with himself, he'd drink his own bath water.'

Simon Hoggart commented: 'Possibly that is a cleaned up version of something similar but more offensive.'

Guardian

A rare piece of wit in the House of Lords:

Lord Walpole asked Foreign Office Minister Lord Triesman: 'I have a daughter in the Foreign Office. Can the FO teach her to speak English now that she has come back after four years in New York?'

Lord Triesman: 'Some tasks may be beyond even the Foreign Office.'

Ephraim Hardcastle, *Daily Mail*

Matt Faber's son was surprised to learn that Margaret Thatcher was elected three times.

'But, didn't everybody hate her?' he asked.

'Well, certainly, many had that view of her, but as many felt as passionately the other way', replied dad.

'Ah,' said the boy. 'Like Marmite.'

Guardian Weekly

Under the headline ONE MILLION IMMIGRANTS GRANTED BRITISH CITIZENSHIP IN PAST DECADE. The Times reported in May 2007 that among the main occupations given by Romanians and Bulgarians was Circus Artiste.

The Times

This is said to be Gordon Brown's favourite joke (he has told it nine times in public in less than a year):

Former U.S. president Ronald Reagan was due to meet Olof Palme, then the Swedish prime minister. Mr Reagan was aware that Palme came from somewhere in Europe and not too far from Russia and asked his advisers:

'Isn't this man a Communist?'

'No Mr President, he's an anti Communist.'

'I don't care what kind of a Communist he is.'

Daily Telegraph

Some samples of 'vexatious requests' made under the Freedom of Information Act:

- The cost of the Prime Minister's make-up.
- The number of eligible bachelors in the Hampshire police force.
- Amount spent on Ferrero Rocher chocolates by the Foreign Office.
- The number of sex acts perpetrated on Welsh sheep.

The Times

Harold Wilson liked to say of Tony Benn that 'he immatures with age'.

Guardian

The suggestion that retiring PM Tony Blair might be given a bicycle as a leaving present should be resisted, writes David Thorpe, of Great Missenden, Buckinghamshire. As a young neighbour of theirs near Durham in the 1960s he was a nuisance riding around ringing his bell.

The Times

Simon Hoggart writes: You could fill a book with quotes wrongly attributed to Winston Churchill. There's no record of the reported occasion when Labour MP Bessie Braddock accused Winston of being drunk and his supposed reply was: 'And you, madam, are ugly. But I shall be sober in the morning.'

Daily Mail

George Bernard Shaw cabled Winston Churchill: 'Have reserved two tickets for my first night. Bring a friend if you have one'. Churchill replied: 'Impossible to come first night. Will come second night if you have one.'

Reader's Digest

In his memoirs, Churchill's wartime driver recalls Winston's predilection for wandering around with nothing on. Once, in the White House, Churchill had just taken a bath and was dictating to his secretary while naked. Roosevelt walked in, but Winston was not embarrassed. He said: 'You see, sir, we have nothing to hide.'

Independent on Sunday

Tory MP Ann Winterton was dismissed from the Shadow Cabinet for telling a racist joke and Richard Ingrams wrote of the very poor quality of politicians' jokes. But he remembered that Winston Churchill could crack a good joke. In his old age Winston was told by a fellow MP that his flies were undone. 'Thank you,' replied the old warrior, 'but a dead bird never falls from the nest'.

Observer

In 1954 Winston Churchill was resisting efforts to persuade him to retire as prime minister. Harold Macmillan remembers that on January 26 Churchill rang at 9.00 am and asked him to go round to Number Ten. 'I found him in bed, with a green budgerigar sitting on his head. A whisky and soda was by his side – of this, the little bird took sips'.

Sunday Times

Churchill wore artificial silk long johns, 'the better to care for the delicate skin on one small part of my anatomy'.

Daily Mail

Before his first meeting with Charles de Gaulle, Churchill was instructed to be ready to kiss the French leader on both cheeks. 'I'll kiss him on all four if you insist,' growled Winston.

Andy Milne, Dilwyn, Hereford.

Daily Telegraph

For Winston Churchill, the underground Cabinet War Rooms used in World War II had two major deficiencies: no flush lavatories and no cellar of decent claret. To the horror of his staff, Churchill's favourite station was the top floor of 10 Downing Street from where he could watch the full fury of the blitz. 'He thought being underground was not a proper place for a Prime Minister to be,' said his grandson, Nicholas Soames, MP.

Guardian

When Churchill was kicked out of office in the first election after World War II his legendary cook Georgina Landemare said: 'I don't know what the world's coming to, but I thought I might make some tea'.

Half an hour before a big dinner, Georgina was often to be found sitting in her kitchen, with everything under control, reading *The Sporting Life*.

The Times

When Nicholas Soames was about six he went into Churchill's working room at Chartwell and said: 'Grandpa, is it true that you are the greatest man in the world?' 'Yes,' said Churchill, 'now bugger off'.

The Times (from a footnote in Roy Jenkins' biography)

Former London Mayor Ken Livingstone escaped censure after likening a Jewish reporter to a concentration camp guard because when the words were spoken he was wearing a cap and thus off duty.

Guardian

Richard Heller, who was Denis Healey's political adviser, tells of the time when Denis referred to Mrs Thatcher 'screaming like a fishwife'. This attracted complaints from fishwives 'to whom he apologised'.

Guardian

Blackpool is often the venue of choice for political annual conferences – but they are small beer to the famous seaside resort, bringing in a mere 10,000 delegates. The real money spinner is the pigeon fanciers' British Homing World Show of the Year, which attracts 25,000 each January (pigeons not included).

The Times

In the summer of 1969 Eric Campbell, of Harrogate, visited a friend who was temporarily renting the house of Roy Jenkins, then Chancellor of the Exchequer. 'Perusing the great man's impressive library I came across *Teach Yourself Economics*.'

The Times

The 3rd Baron Lord Selsdon said that 'after deep research' he had broken down his fellow peers and peeresses into four categories:
- Bought their way in
- Wormed their way in
- Screwed their way in
- And – how did THEY get in?

Daily Mail

Former UK foreign secretary Lord Carrington got into his car to go to a function at Madame Tussaud's waxworks and said to his chauffeur: 'Now to the Chamber of Horrors'. He dozed off and woke up when the car stopped – outside the House of Lords.

Financial Times

Here is the advice from the House of Commons Commission on how to tidy up a broken light bulb:

- Put on protective gloves
- Put on protective mask
- Open sturdy box
- Pick up large fragments and place in box
- Sweep up splinters using stiff card or paper and place in box
- Clean area using damp cloth
- Place damp cloth in box
- Seal sturdy box using tape
- Label contents of box with labels and pen or paper
- Take sealed box to waste removal area and pass to waste disposal contractor

Daily Mail

Flora Edwards read a report on New York's governor meeting a high class call girl in the Mayflower Hotel in Washington. The reporter went on to say that Bill Clinton embraced Monica Lewinsky there, John F Kennedy is rumoured to have used it for extramarital assignations, and 'the Queen and Winston Churchill used the hotel'.

'Whatever is he suggesting?' asks Flora.

Daily Mail

Britain's Secret Intelligence Service was based in 22-storey Century House, not far from Waterloo station. Its location was London's worst kept secret... known only to every taxi driver, tourist guide and KGB agent in the city.

Daily Telegraph

A *Times* reader's request for a collective noun for politicians produced the suggestions 'An ignorance', 'A prattle', 'A thicket', 'A tornado (a spinning mass of hot air)', 'A dissemblance', 'A political asylum', 'A spinney', 'A forest (dense, wooden, parts may die yet remain in place for years)'.

Harold Macmillan once suggested that a suitable collective noun for a gathering of former prime ministers might be 'A lack of principles'.

The Times

Tony Benn once asked Gandhi what he thought of British civilisation. Gandhi told him: 'It would be a good idea'.

Daily Telegraph

While in London a child asked George W. Bush what the White House was like. 'It is white,' he said.

Sunday Telegraph

My seven-year-old niece's autograph book was sent to No.10 and she received a photograph of the Prime Minister with a facsimile signature. She read out to us the accompanying note and it came out as 'a photograph of the Prime Minister with a fake smile.'

Nigel Swann, Derbyshire.

Daily Telegraph

A *Times* reader was told that smoke bombs used for clearing gardens of moles cannot be bought in the UK because of EU rules. But some friends brought some over from France and they did the job. The reader signs off: 'Could we please join the French EU? I'm sick of the British one.'

The Times

CHAPTER 9

ANIMAL MAGIC

**LOST – grey cat. Answers to Lucy
or Here Kitty Kitty...**

In September 2007 it was reported that Chancellor Alistair Darling's cat Sybil had moved into No.10 Downing Street. The Sun remembered how Winston Churchill had a ginger tom called Jock which slept on his bed and attended wartime Cabinet meetings. When he was writing his memoirs Winston had a budgie perched on his head, the cat on his lap and a poodle across his feet.

Sun

Hens have a way of coping with over-amorous cockerels that may be familiar to many women. They give them what they want first thing in the morning to avoid being pestered later, scientists have found.

Daily Telegraph

Advert in local paper: 'LOST – Grey Cat. Answers to Lucy or Here Kitty, Kitty'.

Richard Flaugher, *Reader's Digest*

A white cat in Wolverhampton regularly jumps aboard the number 331 bus and gets off two stops later.

No one knows why he does this, but it may have something to do with the fish and chip shop at its destination.

Independent on Sunday

Percy, a 120-year-old tortoise, keeps neighbours awake by heading a football against his garden fence in Brighton, Sussex.

Sun

Some years ago the Portsmouth Evening News hailed the Queen's successful exhibition of her Jerseys with the headline: MAJOR SHOW AWARD FOR WINDSOR COW.

Portsmouth Evening News

The Great Yarmouth Sea Life Centre has acquired a South American snapping turtle, described as 'a tropical variety with a vicious bite and a temper to match'. It will be known as Prescott.

Norwich Evening News

There's a seagull in Aberdeen which likes to dine at his favourite corner shop. He makes a daily stop there, hopping from foot to foot until staff open the door. Then he strolls in and helps himself to tortilla chips. But not just any kind. Only Chilli Heatwave Doritos will do. He has become a popular tourist attraction and customers have started paying for his chips.

Daily Mail

Pippa, a 17-year-old cockatoo, spent a fortnight trying to hatch some Cadbury Creme eggs at the Nuneaton Wildlife Sanctuary, where they said: 'We'll just leave her until she clicks they are not real. If you try to take one she goes crazy'.

Sunday Times / The Week

Robins have taken to singing at night because humans make too much noise in the daytime.

Guardian

Down Rover! British dog lovers are increasingly giving their pets human names. A survey revealed the top ten names as Ben, Sam, Max, Toby, Holly, Charlie, Lucy, Barney, Bonnie and Sophie.

Top cat names were: Charlie, Tigger, Oscar, Lucy, Soot, Thomas, Poppy, Sophie, Smudge and Molly.

The Times

John Wayne called his dog 'Dog'.

The Times

A Labrador is far more English than the bulldog. It is more English than the crumpets he wolfs and the chintz sofas he hogs. A dog that an Englishman would rather pet than Kylie Minogue's bottom.

Daily Telegraph

Tash, the pub cat at the Salerie Inn in St Peter Port, Guernsey, bears an unfortunate resemblance to Adolf Hitler. Tash has a striking Fuhrer-type black moustache which causes customers to advise: 'Don't mention the paw.'

Daily Mail

A Mayfield, East Sussex, woman bought a birdbath with coins worth £8.20 left on her garden bird table by a crow.

Birmingham Evening Mail

A woman who entered a photograph of her Burmese cat in a 'beautiful pet' competition in Bedford was told that she could not claim the prize she won because the cat had been dead for two years.

Bedfordshire on Sunday

RSPCA inspectors summoned to free an owl trapped in a church tower in Bath called off the rescue when they discovered it was stuffed. It was put there so that customers at a nearby binoculars shop could test their equipment.

Daily Telegraph

A survey of American tourists in Scotland revealed that one in four of them believed that haggis was an animal they could hunt.

Evening Standard

Scientists in Canada and Scotland report that schools of herring communicate by farting. Researchers suspect that herrings hear the bubbles as they are expelled and the noise helps them to form protective shoals at night.

National Geographic News

The way to find lasting love is to take your dog for a walk in the park. Warwick University scientists claim that people who do this are more likely to meet a future partner than anywhere else. Health psychologist June McNicholas said having a dog could increase the chance of getting 'chatted up' by up to 1,000 per cent.

Daily Telegraph

A Jack Russell terrier called Part-X is being trained by its owner to water-ski after learning how to ride a surfboard.

Sun

EXCUSE ME, MISS, IS THAT A CHAMELEON ON YOUR HEAD? *Daily Telegraph* headline on its story about a 17-year-old who tried to get through Customs at Manchester wearing the protected species as a hat.

Daily Telegraph

Cats have recently replaced dogs as the nation's favourite pets and there are over seven million of them – mostly owned by women. Eighty per cent of subscribers to Cats Today magazine are women and editor Jill Reid is convinced that many men are cat lovers, but they would be embarrassed to be seen with a cat magazine. The *Guardian* reports that Jill's own cat, Coco, prefers to snuggle on the chest of her boyfriend Tim and says: 'Tim thinks the explanation is that men's chests are more level'.

Guardian

Dogs top the list of animals used in advertising. Cats come next, although perceived by some as being selfish and cruel. Surprisingly pigs come third, despite 'a reputation for less than pristine personal hygiene'. Researchers found that 'Britons have an almost ludicrous affinity to pigs. If you go into almost any home in the country they are there – in figurines, pictures or just piggybanks'.

Daily Telegraph

A hamster was seen bowling along inside its toy exercise ball on the hard shoulder of the M6.

Independent on Sunday

Environmental health officers in Barbegh, Suffolk, received a complaint from a woman that a neighbour's horse was urinating too loudly. The complaint was among the top ten of their most unusual calls.

Sunday Times

A lost pet tortoise was found safe and well on a motorway having crawled one-and-a-half miles in three weeks. Freddy, owned by Wendy Passell of Otterbourne, near Winchester, was seen plodding south on the M3 having managed an average speed of 0.0034mph. Proud Mrs Passell said: 'People don't realise how hyperactive Freddie is.'

Evening Standard

A survey in *Our Dogs* magazine found a bull terrier which swallowed a bottle cap, a toy car and some wire and some cling film. It was operated on, the objects were removed and the dog was put on a drip. It ate the drip.

Sunday Times

Legendary actress Sarah Bernhard had a pet alligator which died after she fed him too much champagne. And her boa constrictor died after swallowing a cushion.

Daily Mail

Bathers swam towards a huge basking shark (they can be around 40ft long and weigh up to seven tonnes) which appeared off Porthcurno beach in Cornwall.

Lifeguards were quickly on the scene – but they were there to protect the shark, not the bathers. Basking sharks are a protected species which feed on plankton and are regarded as harmless. 'We try to keep people away from them', said one of the guards.

The Times

A 1997 edition of *The Times* reported:

The royal pets include a number of 'dorgis' – crosses between the Queen's corgis and Princess Margaret's dachshunds.

Royal photographer Norman Parkinson was having lunch at the Palace one day and had the temerity to ask how the breeds could couple successfully, considering their different stature.

'Oh,' said the Queen, 'it's really very simple. We have a little brick.'

The Times

A Kennel Club official commented: 'The dachshund was evolved to chase badgers down holes and corgis to round up cattle. If anyone loses a herd of cattle down a badger hole, dorgis are just the dogs to get them out.'

The Times

J. Mervyn Williams, of Huddersfield, remembers calling into a pub in Wales in the early 1960s when the locals were discussing how much it cost having sheep neutered by vets 'since old Edwards died'. He asked them if he could make a good living if he set up doing the job old Edwards did.

They asked him: 'Have you got your own teeth?'

Daily Mail

Dogs and pubs rival the weather as subjects of conversation among the English. The *Daily Telegraph* had a whole raft of letters on them:
- **Children should be barred from pubs, but dogs are an essential accessory.**
- **Dogs are grotesquely over-privileged manure machines and should be kept out of pubs.**
- **Dogs are never the pub bore.**
- **Landlords who want to ban dogs should be banned from running pubs.**

Daily Telegraph

Warwickshire Fire Brigade swung into action in response to a 999 call. It sent three fire engines (with five men to each engine) and two men with a rubber dinghy. They travelled 35 miles to a drainage tunnel at Earlswood Lakes, near Solihull – and rescued a trapped duck.

BBC News / Guardian

Sue Baines, of Quernmore, Lancashire, had a cat called Geoffrey which was known as Geoffrey Boycat.

Daily Telegraph

Under the headline WHY YOU REALLY CAN'T CALL YOUR CAT KEITH, Christopher Howse informs us of some oddball monikers humans have given to their cats.

Thomas Hardy had one called Kiddleywinkempoops, and many a poor cat is called Astrophe and Aclysm (or anything else that begins with 'cat').

Florence Nightingale had Bismarck and Disraeli.

Jock and Margate belonged to Winston Churchill.

Ernest Hemingway had Fats, Crazy Christian and Friendless Brother.

It is said that Thomas Hardy's ashes were to be buried at Westminster Abbey and his heart in his Dorset village. The heart was left for a few minutes in the kitchen in a tea towel. His cat ate it. The tale is denied, but the story will not go away.

Daily Telegraph

Strange names for animals reminded Marjorie Stratton, of Chippenham, Wiltshire, of a chap who had a horse called Business. His wife was able to reply truthfully to demanding phones calls that her husband was away on Business when he was enjoying a day on his hunter.

Daily Telegraph

It's not mice that elephants are afraid of... it's bees. Despite their thick skins and size advantage, elephants turn tail and flee at the sound of a swarm of bees according to research in Kenya.

Guardian

A Huddersfield man has had to change his mobile phone ring tone five times because Billy, his blue-fronted Amazon parrot, learns to copy it. Billy waits until his owner is out of the room before pretending to be an incoming call – then laughs when he dashes in to answer it.

Daily Telegraph

A car thief had a swift change of heart when he was confronted by a Great Dane called Diesel which had been asleep in the back of the car. As the thief drove off Diesel – nine stone in weight and six foot tall on his hind legs – sat up and the driver jerked to a halt and fled. The car owner said that his car did not have an alarm. 'Who needs one when you've got the Hound of the Baskervilles in your back seat?'

The Times

This reminded Richard Littlejohn of the man who parked his Mondeo near Anfield football ground. He was approached by a gang of scallies offering to mind his car for a fiver.

'No need,' he said. 'My Rottweiler's in the back'.

To which the response was: 'Can he put out fires?'

Daily Mail

In February 2008 the *Daily Mail* carried a picture of Shirley Neeley's fridge full of hibernating tortoises. Mrs Neeley, who runs the Jersey-based Tortoise Sanctuary, said: 'It's much easier to maintain a constantly cool temperature with a fridge than it is with our ever-warming climate.'

One night a guest went in search of wine and was stunned to find the main contents of the fridge were alive and had four legs. But there WAS also a bottle of wine because, said Mrs Neeley, 'It helps to stabilise the temperature'.

Daily Mail

CHAPTER 10

NANNY STATE

**Clown ordered to stop blowing
bubbles for children...**

A Premium Bond holder rang to give them his new address. 'Sorry, sir, we cannot take it over the telephone for security reasons', they said. 'We will have to send you a form.'

The bond holder gave the address to which the form should be sent... his new address. The Premium Bond people arranged to send a form to his new address so that he could fill it in to tell them his new address.

Sunday Telegraph

Someone put up the idea of withdrawing packets of ten cigarettes to discourage teenagers from smoking.

Maureen McKinlay, of Cardiff, responded: 'Brilliant. When packets of five were withdrawn I bought ten and increased my consumption almost overnight.'

Daily Telegraph

Clown Barney Baloney has had to stop blowing bubbles for children after being warned that youngsters might slip on the bubbles' residue.

Said Barney: 'The fun is being taken out of children's lives by bureaucracy. Kids eat ice cream and jelly and that gets on the floor and is slippy. Do they want them to stop eating those?'

Daily Telegraph

When a Health and Safety Officer visited Pat Robbins' Berkshire game hatchery he saw a ladder propped up against a 10-foot high grain bin and said: 'I don't want anyone climbing that ladder until it has been secured from the top'. The inspector left, somewhat discomfited, after being asked: 'How do we get up there to secure it?'

Sunday Telegraph

The Queen is a confirmed non-smoker, but she is also a great libertarian and has no time for political correctness. She always makes cigarettes available for guests. She also refuses to wear a hard hat when she is riding and she refuses to wear a seatbelt when she travels by car.

Sunday Telegraph

After visiting Sunningdale Ladies' Golf Club a Health and Safety official said the sand pits would have to be fenced in. The sand pits to which the official referred are known to golfers as bunkers.

Ephraim Hardcastle, *Daily Mail*

Tracey Barnes from Claverham, Somerset, was told by the Passport Office that she could not use a photograph of her nine-month old baby son because it showed him bare-chested.

Daily Telegraph

Police called in to investigate the vandalising of stained glass windows at Middleton Parish Church near Rochdale didn't get close-up pictures of the damage because 'they didn't have specialised ladder training'.

Daily Mail

Children were banned from taking part in a 2007 Llandudno Donkey Derby. Instead, cuddly toys were tied to the donkeys and the children ran behind. 'Absolutely ridiculous,' said donkey owner Phil Talbort. 'The races have been held here for 40-odd years and no child has ever been injured. The donkeys enjoy the Derby so much that they'll just go on their own.'

The glamorous granny and bonny baby contests went ahead without any recorded fatalities.

North Wales Pioneer and others

Reactions to the widespread smoking ban which came into force in England on 1 July 2007 included:

- At the Old King's Arms at Horsforth, near Leeds, the landlord said: 'We've had one or two regulars vowing that they won't come back. But give it a week or two of them sitting at home staring at the wife. They'll be back.' *The Times*

- In London, comedian and writer Liam Mullone bought a converted hearse and spent the day driving from pub to pub offering shelter to smokers shivering in doorways. *The Times*

- The *Daily Mail* had a picture of three men smoking at the Smokers Arms in Grimsby – outside in the cold.

- £2billion is the estimated cost of smoking to the NHS. £9.5billion is the profit to the Treasury made from tobacco taxes in 2006. *Daily Mail*

- Lap dancers in a Brighton club slipped outdoors in their undies for a drag and Arabic smokers took their hubble bubble pipes outside in London. *Sun*

- Strippers will dance at the Crown in Knaphill, Surrey, to entice smokers to keep using the pub. *News of the World*

- Llanelli cemetery in South Wales became a no-smoking area because it is a workplace for gravediggers.

- A quote from the *Guardian:* 'I smoke 100 to 120 cigs a day. The ban will kill us'.

Firemen were barred from taking down festival bunting in Ampthill, Bedfordshire because they were not allowed to use ladders to under Health and Safety rules. A local fire chief said: 'The world's gone mad'.

Sun (which printed the story alongside its 'You Couldn't Make It Up' logo.)

CHAPTER 11

FOOD FOR THOUGHT

A diner at a Slug & Lettuce found a slug in her lettuce...

Oyster grower is besieged with orders after claiming that he feeds Viagra to his bivalves.

Independent on Sunday

David Dimbleby revealed that he had a great aunt who added her cigarette ash to her porridge. It improved the taste, she said.

Sun

Eamon Butler, of the Adam Smith Institute, declares: 'Bismarck said that if you like laws or sausages you should never watch either being made.'

Daily Mail

Anthony Danson, 43, won the World Pie Eating Championship in Wigan in 2005. He demolished seven large meat and potato pies in three minutes (that's one in every 25.714 seconds). This was after eating three pies in a warm-up session 20 minutes before the competition. None of the other competitors managed more than three.

'Were it seven?' he said. 'I thought it were six.' Mr Danson explained that he was on a seafood diet: 'If I see food, I eat it.'

Daily Telegraph

Trading standards jobsworths in Weymouth, Dorset, have ordered local baker Val Temple to rename her novelty Robin Tarts because they do not contain robin. Her Paradise Slice has to be reclassified as it does not come from paradise. And her comical Pig Tarts came under the axe because they do not contain pork.

60-year-old Val says: 'I've been selling all these cakes for 16 years. They are a bit of fun and my customers love them.'

The *Sun* commented: 'May we suggest that Val adds warning labels such as 'Shepherd's Pie – Contains No Shepherds.'

Sun

Scotsman headline: Tv Ads Boost Eating of Obese Children by 130%. Best with ketchup and a mild chutney, comments the *Guardian*'s Duncan Campbell.

Guardian

Dr Rick Jolly, of Crafthole, Cornwall, recalls how, 'in the Commando world we always carried a cardboard tube filled with curry powder. The Royal Marines' delightful nickname for this absolutely essential and taste-making dietary supplement was "Go-faster dust"'.

Daily Telegraph

Grand Tory MP Lady Nancy Astor splendidly advised the poor in the 1930's how to make nutritious soup from potato and carrot peelings. But author Pamela Horn reveals in her book, *Life Below Stairs*, that when Lady Astor went on holiday she took one of her own dairy cows with her to ensure a regular supply of her usual milk.

Observer

A prisoner was granted legal aid to sue the Home Secretary because he was refused a second helping of rhubarb crumble in the jail canteen.

Daily Mail

More people in Britain are employed in Indian restaurants than in the mining, shipping and steel industries combined - and we now export chicken tikka masala to India, while they export hi-tech software to us.

Guardian

When Oscar-winning actress Gwyneth Paltrow complained that British men appeared to be scared to ask her out, the *Daily Telegraph* reported a 'Stockport lad' offering to take her Up North for chicken in a basket. 'But don't call on Saturdays. I'm usually out watching Man City'.

Daily Telegraph

Stories about a Scottish delicacy – the 1,000 calorie deep fried chocolate sandwich – brought a warning from the Sun: It would take two hours of sex to work off the calorific effect of the 'Suicide Sarnie'.

Sun

On a train from Kemble to Paddington I saw this message written on a paper napkin in the buffet car: 'Would the last person on duty tonight please moisten the ginger cake as it is past its sell-by date.' Kyrle Arscott, Ashton Keynes, Wiltshire.

Daily Telegraph

A *Daily Telegraph* reader from Dawlish Water, Devon, bought a jar of chutney from Tesco carrying the 'Best Before' date of 4 June 2163. He says he is considering leaving it to one of his children as an heirloom.

Daily Telegraph

The soggy and curly British Rail sandwich was the subject of meticulous culinary precision according to a 30-year-old document unearthed in National Railway Museum of York. It taught employees to use only three quarters of an ounce of cheese, two-thirds of an ounce of luncheon meat, cress or sardine and no more than a quarter ounce of gherkin. At least a third of the sandwich filling was to be stacked on the centre of the bread to make it look attractive and well-filled.

Independent

Claims that the Cornish Pasty was invented in Devon continue to anger Cornwall. Gary Spires, of Penzance, Cornwall, writes: 'If Devon invented the pasty then Cornwall has done something wonderful to it – it's as if Devon invented the toilet seat and Cornwall came up with the idea of a hole in the middle'.

Western Morning News

The league table of British foods which have had the biggest impact on worldwide cuisine:

1. Worcester sauce
2. Cheddar cheese
3. Yorkshire pudding
4. Clotted cream
5. Black pudding
6. English mustard
7. Scones
8. Salad cream
9. Mint sauce
10. Jellied eels

Daily Telegraph

Mrs. A. Maurice's first efforts at baking bread were not a total success. When a TV ad came on extolling a bread 'Just like mother makes', her children pleaded: 'Please don't buy it Mummy.'

Daily Mail

Dr K. R. Whittington, of Cambridge, attempted to cook porridge in a coffee percolator when in student digs in the 50s. His landlady was not amused when the contents erupted 'volcano fashion' into her piano on which the percolator was standing.

The Times

A *Times* reader expressed surprise when his electric kettle came with instructions that it was to be used only for boiling water. His letter was followed by one from hotelier Martin Armistead, of Ickford, Buckinghamshire, saying: 'I have seen kettles in hotel bedrooms that have been used to boil eggs and even cook a curry. Perhaps the most imaginative was the trouser press used to reheat pizza'.

The Times

Mark Brightman told of a student who attempted to heat a can of baked beans in an electric kettle.

The Times

A packet of nuts on a flight to the US carried the instruction: 'Open the packet. Eat nuts.'

Jo Morrison, London. *The Times*

The question is: Why, after eating asparagus, does one's pee smell so extraordinary? One London club had for many years a notice reading: 'During the asparagus season, members are requested not to relieve themselves into the umbrella stand.'

Guardian

My husband gave up on the bread machine immediately he realised that the bread did not come out sliced and wrapped in polythene.

Gloria Gillott from Cambridge in *The Times*

A jar of mincemeat I bought carried the following message: 'The contents are sufficient for a pie for six persons or 12 small tarts'

David Morris-Marsham, SW12. *The Times*

A recipe of breathtaking complexity for making beans on toast comes from the Heinz stable. It requires a slice of bread 1.56cm thick from an uncut white loaf, 9.3g of unsalted butter stored at 16.8 degrees centigrade and 280g of beans heated to 64 degrees centigrade. Use an oven grill and not a toaster and when the desired colour is reached, leave to stand for 1 minute 8 seconds. Spread the butter to achieve a uniform seepage of 2.13mm.

Guardian

Lee and Mary Humphrey, both 84, have eaten at McDonald's every day for 17 years. They even moved house to be within walking distance of their local branch in Eastbourne, Sussex. They turn up at 11am without fail for a double hamburger and fries to share. They have had the same meal 6,000 times.

Sun, under the headline: I'M LOVIN' IT

Basil Marcuson writes to Simon Hoggart about a family he saw on the Tube. Mother and father were seriously obese and junior was well on his way. He heard the mother say: 'No, you can't have any more sweets. You'll spoil your McDonald's.'

Guardian

In a week when newspapers were full of scary stories about how salt is bad for you, one of Britain's oldest women celebrated her 110th birthday. To the undoubted horror of health police, Mary Brown, of Godalming, Surrey, put her longevity down to having an inquiring mind, not driving, and enjoying plenty of salt on all her food.

Daily Telegraph

Another defiant old timer celebrated her 100th birthday with a cake decorated with candles spelling out 1-0-0. When the candles were lit, Beatrice Langley, of Croydon, stepped forward and lit her fag off one of them. She has been a smoker since she was eight. STILL FULL OF PUFF, said the *Guardian* headline.

Guardian

The world's poshest grocery store – Fortnum and Mason – introduced baked beans in their Piccadilly emporium in 1886.

The Times

One of Terry Wogan's fans came across a Senior Citizen Special Breakfast: two eggs, bacon, hash browns and toast, £1.99.

A woman ordered the Special, but said: 'I don't want the eggs'.

The waitress said that in that case the breakfast would be £2.49 – 'because you're ordering a la carte'.

'OK', said the customer, 'I'll take the Special at £1.99'.

'How do you want your eggs?'

'Raw and in the shell', said the customer.

She was served the raw eggs as requested – and took them home.

Sunday Telegraph

Fanny Craddock, once the grand dame of TV cookery, campaigned against artificial flavourings and fertilisers. She fed her tomatoes on a diet of tea and pee (dubbed Madam's Tonic).

Daily Telegraph

Steve Hawkes, retail correspondent of *The Times*, writes: 'Britons are embracing the Government's five-a-day message as never before – that's one cheeseburger, medium fries, a Coke, ice cream and, go on then, chicken nuggets on the side.'

The Times

In February 2008 Billy Bunter, the bespectacled fat owl of the remove at Greyfriars School, became 100 years old.

Despite being the living embodiment of pride, envy, avarice, greed, sloth, wrath and gluttony, he still has his own fan club, known as the Friars. The club celebrated the centenary at a meal heavy with pies and puddings. Bunter would have called it tuck 'and wouldn't be satisfied until he had gorged on everything on offer'.

The Times

CHAPTER 12

WEDDED BLISS

**A man wanting a happy marriage
should keep his chequebook open and his
mouth shut...**

Divorcing couples are now spending more time fighting over who gets custody of the family pet than over furniture or the hi-fi.

Independent on Sunday

It was reported that Whitney Houston's song 'I Will Always Love You' is the top choice for the first dance for newly weds.

Duncan Mackinven, of Romford, Essex, says he can only assume that they have never listened to the lyrics, which include 'We both know I'm not what you need'.

Daily Telegraph

In an article headlined 12 Ways to Enjoy Life for Longer the 8th item was:

Nag Your Husband:
Gerald drops off to sleep after lunch and says 'Winston Churchill always had a power nap'. I say 'Yes, well he had power and a country to run. All you've got to remember is to take the bins out.'

Women who nag their husbands are less likely to die of heart disease. Do you need another reason?

'It's fun.'

Daily Telegraph

Spotted in a parish magazine by Mrs Jean Gelder, of Gainsborough, Lincolnshire: 'Irving Benson and Jessica Carter were married on October 24. So ends a friendship that began in their schooldays'.

Daily Mail

Rosemary Heaversedge, of Shrewsbury, reports that there was a time when 'Strangers in the Night' was the song played for the bride and groom.

Daily Telegraph

Groucho Marx on men: 'A husband wanting a happy marriage should keep his cheque book open and his mouth shut'.

James Thurber on women: 'I hate them because they always know where things are'.

W. C. Fields said that a woman drove him to drink and he didn't have the decency to thank her.

Nancy Astor said to Winston Churchill: 'If I were married to you I'd put poison in your coffee'. Churchill replied: 'If you were my wife I would drink it'.

Mae West said: 'His mother should have thrown him away and kept the stork'.

Extracts from *The Wicked Wit of Insults* by Maria Leach (Michale O'Mara £5.99)
Daily Mail

Referring to a device which prevents drivers exceeding the speed limit, Richard Fuller, of Salisbury, wrote: 'I have one. We have been married for 24 years.'

The Times

Cherie Blair, wife of the former Prime Minister, tells of the day he proposed: 'We went on holiday in 1979 to Tuscany... we were leaving to come home and I was cleaning the toilet... I was on my knees and he just announced that maybe we should get married. It was terribly romantic.'

Sunday Telegraph

The three Douglas sisters (Agnes, 87, Peggy, 86, and Mary, 84, originally of Sittingbourne, Kent) have clocked up 185 years of wedded bliss. They have been congratulated by the Queen for all reaching their diamond wedding anniversaries, and Mary said: 'I could manage another 60 years'.

Daily Mail

Joseph Smith played 'Nearer My God to Thee' on the harmonium while one of his wives was drowning in the next room.

Keith Waterhouse 'looking back on days of perfect murder' in the *Daily Mail*

In the first year of our marriage I sent my husband a Valentine. He spent all day trying to guess who had sent it. In 45 years I have never sent him another. Elizabeth Ditton, Suffolk.

The Times

Britain's 'ugliest granny' celebrated 60 years of marriage in 2007. Kath Taylor, 81, was twice crowned World Gurning Champion at Cumbria's Egremont Crab Fair. Her husband James, 84, reckons she is a stunner and says: 'She's a little beauty, even when pulling those funny faces.'

His love did not wane when Kath lost her teeth and took up gurning. 'It's fun,' she says, 'but you can get tired of frightening children in the street.'

Sun

In 2007 James Mason (93) and Peggy Clarke (84) of Devon became Britain's oldest wedding couple – with a combined age of 177. They had both agreed that there was no point in a long engagement.

Mason said it was a perfect match: 'She was after my body and I was after her money. And I've always wanted to marry a younger woman.'

They met at a Paignton day centre where he began the romance with the bewhiskered old time favourite: 'Do you come here often?'

Three days later he popped the question, 'But not on bended knees because of his creaky joints', reported the *Guardian*.

Daily Mail

Writing about attacks on the clergy, the Venerable George Austin of York reported: 'I once received a death threat from a man because I had given him 25 years of misery by conducting his marriage service'.

The Times

Police received a 999 call from a husband complaining that his wife would not cook him an evening meal because she was decorating.

Daily Mirror

Ten days after her wedding, a 20-year-old Arbroath bride found her husband in bed with her 44-year-old mother. Divorce followed and then the husband married the mother – with his first wife acting as bridesmaid. Bride number one said: 'He never apologised, but everyone makes mistakes. I've lost a husband, but gained a father.

Independent on Sunday

'Wedding dress size 16 – £75. Worn once. Big mistake.' Seen in Kettering local paper.

Daily Mail

'Beautiful ivory wedding dress, size 10, never worn due to pregnancy.'

Rugby Observer

With many more people going in for serial monogamy these days, the greeting card industry has had to change. There are cards addressed to 'dad and his wife' and to 'mother and her partner'.

Independent on Sunday

A Yorkshireman asked his wife where she would like to be buried. She replied: 'On top o' thee.'
Bernard Breckon, Beverley, Yorkshire.

The Times

Growing numbers of bridegrooms are choosing women to be their 'best man'. A best woman is considered to be less likely to organise a stag night that ends up with a plastered groom being tied to a lamppost minus his trousers. She is less likely to deliver a speech revealing the groom's more outrageous bachelor indiscretions. But she must not try to look more pretty than the bride and must not let the bride see her trying on the wedding ring.

The Times

A man filed for divorce because his wife left him this note: 'Gone to the bridge club. There'll be a recipe for your dinner at seven o'clock on Channel 2'.

Reader's Digest

It was reported that women spend a total of three years in their lifetime dressing up to go out – but it turned out to be nothing new. John Dyer, of Otham, Kent, recalled that Gladstone said that he was able to read *War and Peace* in the time that he had spent waiting for Mrs Gladstone to put on her hat.

Daily Telegraph

CHAPTER 13

WHAT'S UP, DOC?

**Going bald? Try rubbing in
some chicken dung...**

Jane Morrison, of Crieff, Perth and Kinross, writes
of her father who was a GP on a Hebridean island.
A crofter complained of a painful spine and was
asked if he had undertaken any strenuous activities.
'I suppose,' he said, 'it could have been when I
lifted a sack of peat on to the wife's back.'

Reader's Digest

Lottery winners Tony and Greta Dodd (67 and 69 years
old) of Wallasey, Merseyside, knew exactly what to do
first with their £2,438,155 prize. Get four new knee joints.

Daily Mail

Two patients a week leave hospital with surgical instruments still inside them. The list of lost items includes swabs, a catheter, a metal clip and a contraceptive coil.

Pensioner Victor Hutchinson spent three months with a two-inch scalpel blade in his chest after a heart operation in Plymouth.

Daily Mail

The NHS surgery used by Brian Binns, of Loughborough, Leicestershire, has a wall calendar supplied by the local undertaker.

Daily Telegraph

News of yet another cure for baldness hit the headlines on 17 May 2007, and The Times reminded readers that Hippocrates recommended a blend of pigeon droppings, cumin, horseradish and beetroot. The Ancient Egyptians had a remedy which included toe of dog and hoof of ass.

The Times

Back in the 1940s Jenny Parkin's grandfather suffered a coronary thrombosis at the age of 50. His doctor told him to give up golf and carry on smoking.

He followed the advice and lived to be 93.

The Times

After being told that he had only 12 months to live John Brandrick, of Newquay, Cornwall, gave up his job, stopped paying his mortgage, helped out his family financially, gave away his clothes and enjoyed spending the rest of his life savings. He planned his funeral, keeping just one suit, a shirt and a tie to be buried in. He then learned that he had non-fatal pancreatitis and not pancreatic cancer – but was penniless and forced to sell his house.

His verdict on the past 12 months? Get a second opinion.

Daily Telegraph

The 1654 book prompted the *Independent on Sunday* to look at other 'cures' for baldness which have cropped up over the years:

- **Former Labour MP Bryan Gould claimed that hanging upside down (increasing the flow of blood to the scalp) led to a 50% regrowth on his receding bonce.**
- **Hippocrates recommended a blend of pigeon droppings, cumin, horseradish and beetroot.**
- **Queen Victoria was known to drink silver birch wine, made from the rising sap, to cure her baldness.**

Independent on Sunday

According to *The Path-Way to Health*, published back in 1654 when Oliver Cromwell was ruling England, it seems that no self-respecting male's medicine chest was complete without supplies of cat dung, snail blood and chicken droppings. They were recommended as remedies for everything from bad breath to baldness and fatness to flatulence.

The advice for getting rid of unwanted hair was to 'take hard cat dung, beat it to a powder, temper it with strong vinegar, then use it to wash the place where you would have no hair grow.'

For curing stinking breath wash the mouth out with water and vinegar followed by a concoction of aniseed, mint and cloves sodden in wine.

For a stench under the armpits, pluck away the hairs and wash with white wine and rosewater.

Going bald? Try rubbing in some chicken dung and/or snail blood.

Daily Mail

A Perthshire health centre was accused of insensitivity after issuing cards to patients that included an advert for the town's funeral director.

The Times

If you think today's adverts need to be taken with a pinch of salt, the *Daily Mail* reproduces some glorious golden oldies:

- Groves Tonic 'Makes Children and Adults as Fat as Pigs' – 1890s
- Joy's Cigars Cure Asthma (with a picture of a sophisticated lady puffing on one) – 1890s
- The Doctors' Special Rum (Prescribed by the Medical Profession) – 1900
- Whiteway's Woodbine Blend Dry Cider for Rheumatism and Gout – 1920
- A 6d bottle of Mason's Wine Essence will make One Gallon of Delicious Wine for Children's Parties – 1900
- And a very pretty girl with a low cut dress advertises Page Woodcock's Wind Pills.

Daily Mail

The doctor giving D. S. Busfield, of Yelverton, Devon, a medical examination admitted that he found taking exercise boring. He said that, if he felt the need, he took his gin and tonic standing up.

Daily Telegraph

Message seen on a wall at a Middlesex Hospital: 'The only difference between this place and the Titanic is that they had a band.'

Guardian

In the Colonial Police Service our medical adviser insisted hands should be washed before having a pee, on the grounds that 'you should know where your willy has been, but not always your hands'.

John S. Wright, Macclesfield, Cheshire.

Independent

A student who rushed for help after seeing a woman fall down the steps of Leeds General Infirmary was told by the Accident and Emergency staff to phone for an ambulance.

Yorkshire Evening Post

Recent letters on the marking of body parts before surgery reminded me of my husband's bunion operation. With a felt-tip pen a nurse drew an arrow near his ankle 'to show the surgeon which foot to operate on.' My husband pointed out that he actually only had the one leg.

Helen Hawes, Tunbridge Wells. *Daily Telegraph*

A man went into Leeds Infirmary for a heart by-pass. Part of a leg vein was removed to replace a blocked artery. This meant that a tattoo on his leg, which used to read 'I love women' ended up reading 'I love men'.

Independent on Sunday

In one recent year almost one million people were admitted to UK hospitals as a result of unfortunate and often unusual incidents (costing the NHS some £1billion). Department of Health statistics show that:

- 51 people were bitten or crushed by reptiles
- 22 were bitten by a rat
- 190 had 'come into contact with plant thorns, spines and sharp leaves'
- 369 had fallen foul of lawnmowers
- 3,038 were injured through 'contact with a non-powered hand drill'
- 389 were admitted after crashing their bicycle into a stationary object
- 31 children under 14 got on a motorcycle and crashed into a car
- 24 were burnt by 'ignition or melting of nightwear'
- 754 were scalded by hot tap water
- 189 needed treatment after 'foreign objects' were accidentally left in their bodies during surgical and medical care.
- Lightning struck 65 times – but not in the same place twice.

Times / Evening Standard

As a medical student I was baffled by the abbreviation BNOR, but discovered from a nurse in the obstetric unit that it meant: 'Bowels not opened regularly.'

Bernard Gaston, Hale, Cheshire. *The Times*

As a retired vet I have also come across useful acronyms. D.M.I.T.O stands for 'dog more intelligent than owner.'

Mike Godsal, Aylesbury, Buckinghamshire.
The Times

A West of England ambulance service, concerned about Britons overeating, ordered an ambulance capable of carrying patients weighing 55 stone.

Independent on Sunday

A disabled woman who says she was healed miraculously after years in a wheelchair could not get her disability payments cancelled because the government does not recognise miracles.

Daily Telegraph

CHAPTER 14

DRIVEN TO DISTRACTION

**Man reaches 65mph in his
mother-in-law's wheelchair after fitting
it with a jet engine...**

It is an age-old truth that anyone who drives slower
than you is an idiot and anyone who drives faster
than you is a lunatic.

Nicholas Ord, Guildford. *The Times*

'I have today received an offer of car insurance. This
includes an invitation to receive the offer in large print
or Braille'.

J. R. C. Sharp of Montrose, Scotland. *The Times*

Police stopped a motorist on the A1 near Colesworth,
Lincs, and arrested him for drink-driving after
noticing that he had only three wheels on his car.

Daily Telegraph

An elderly woman driver who was involved in a crash near Bridport, Dorset, was found to be wearing oven gloves.

Dorset Echo

Some years ago, our student-laden Morris Minor was stopped by a policeman hunting for a robber. We were terrified lest he should spot the Guinness beer bottle label we had standing in for a tax disc. Questions over, he thanked us for our co-operation and, as we breathed sighs of relief, added: 'I'm a Mackeson man myself. Drive carefully, lads'.

Terry O'Brien, London N3. *The Times*

A *Times* reader from Loughborough advised English visitors to Rome that the only safe way to use a pedestrian crossing there is to mingle with a group of nuns. 'Seemingly, Italian drivers regard it as unlucky to run over a nun.'

The Times

Owners of pink and yellow cars are twice as likely to be victims of road rage as drivers of vehicles in other colours – RAC survey.

Sunday Telegraph

We have got a new car journey game – 'Spot the Speed Camera'. Each time a child spots one they get 10p. It is a lot cheaper than a £40 fine and keeps the children amused for the whole journey.

David Harding, Lincoln.
The Times

A baby born on the way to hospital has been named Mondeo after the car that took him there.

Sun

A Teignmouth, Devon, man was given a two year Asbo after tricking women into taking off their tights. He pretended he wanted them to repair his fan belt.

The Times

In reviewing the new edition of the Penguin Dictionary of *Modern Humorous Quotations* the British press showed a marked preference for this one from the wicked Irish pen of P. J. O'Rourke: 'There are a number of sexual devices which increase sexual arousal, particularly in women. Chief among these is the Mercedes-Benz 380SL'.

The Times

'I have always understood that a gentleman was one who could change gear in an Austin Seven without getting his face slapped'.

Rear Admiral J. A. L. Myres, Kennington, Oxon.
Daily Telegraph

Kelvin MacKenzie's column carried a picture of a RAC breakdown truck rescuing an AA van.

Sun

An Automobile Association report shattered male egos by claiming that women make better drivers. Readers of *The Times* fought back with:

'The ruling on women drivers is quite correct. There is no better driver than my wife, especially when she is in the passenger seat and I am at the controls.' R. W. Davis Foster, High Wycombe, Buckinghamshire.

'My husband tells me his driving is incomparable – when I am not with him.' Caroline Charles-Jones, Newport, Pembrokeshire.

'Whilst driving my wife and her mother on a particularly fraught journey, I was eventually forced to ask my wife: "Who is driving this car, you or your mother?"' Ged Clarke, Birkdale, Southport.

'Many years ago I was talking to my mother while we were sitting in the back of the car, my father driving, when she interrupted me, saying: "Just a minute, dear. Just let me get round this corner."' John Hodgkin, Steyning, West Sussex.

The Times

Britain's drivers run over an average 273 hedgehogs every day.

Sun

Postman Pat has ended up on a list of 'dangerous drivers' in an analysis of cartoon characters who would not be welcomed by insurers. Top of the Churchill insurance company's list of Toon Terrors is:

- Dick Dastardly, of Wacky Races, who 'would struggle to find anybody to insure him in real life'.

- Second most uninsurable cartoon character is Homer Simpson – guilty of road rage, sleeping behind the wheel, obesity, poor eyesight and a tendency to eat doughnuts while driving.

- Noddy is 5th – guilty of driving into Big Ear's bike and illegally using his car as a taxi.

- Postman Pat, who carries too many expensive items, is 8th.

The Times

The bad news is that police drivers have caused more than £2.3million worth of damage to their police cars – while reversing. The worst news is that the cost of repairs comes out of taxes because insurance premiums and excesses are so high that police forces do not claim for the damage.

Daily Telegraph

Items left behind by drivers returning vehicles have included: stockings and suspenders, a shop dummy, used nappies, false teeth, a bag of fish and chips and a dead goat.

Fleet News, which monitors the world of company cars.

The following are genuine statements from insurance forms:

- The guy was all over the road. I had to swerve a number of times before I hit him.
- In an attempt to kill a fly, I drove into a telephone pole.
- The pedestrian had no idea which direction to run, so I ran over him.
- Coming home, I turned into the wrong drive and collided with a tree I don't have.

Reg O'Donaghue, London SE 17.

Daily Mail

Norwich Union has a collection of the most novel claims made by drivers. Among them: 'A herd of cows licked my car and damaged the paintwork.'

Independent on Sunday

In August 2004 at RAF Barkston Heath in Lincolnshire, Guiseppe Canella reached a speed of 65mph in his mother in law's wheel chair – after fitting it with a small Rolls-Royce jet engine.

Sunday Telegraph

Insects in cars cause 500,000 crashes a year.

Independent on Sunday

David Page, 40, dug up an object in Coltishall, Norfolk. It was a sort of canister with a button on top. He accidentally pressed down the button and then feared it might be a World War II mine which would explode if he released the button. He wrapped masking tape around his thumb to keep it in place and used his mobile to raise the alarm. Police arrived, packed his arm – and the canister – in a barrel of sand and told him: 'Do not move.' Roads were cordoned off within a two-mile radius. A woman police officer said everything would be OK and David said to her: 'You're not the one holding the bomb.' David kept the button depressed for four hours before bomb disposal experts identified the object as part of a Citroen's hydraulic suspension system. He said later: 'It sounds funny, but it was absolutely horrendous.'

Sun, Guardian, Daily Mail

The DVLA keeps a censorial eye on car number plates and tries to stop possible naughty ones leaking out.

TE57 CLE and BA57 ARD have been blue pencilled. But some which slipped through the system are up for sale:

- PEN 15 (£99,995)
- WHO2 LAY (£3,695)
- FKU 778 (5,500)
- 1CUM (£40,395)
- ORG 45IM (6,599)
- R4 NDY (55,000)

Independent on Sunday

CHAPTER 15

NOT DEAD, JUST RESTING

**Epitaph for promiscuous actress:
At last she sleeps alone**

Derek Honey, of Witney, Oxfordshire, spotted this in the obituary column of the *Oxford Mail*:

'God bless you and keep you from all of your family'.

Daily Mail

Mrs Rickard, of Leigh-on-Sea, Essex, saw this in the Leigh-on-Sea Advertiser after a donation was made to a local hospital: 'My husband died last year in this ward and this is our way of saying Thank You'.

Leigh-on-Sea Advertiser

The identity of a headless corpse found in a wood near Liskeard, Cornwall, will not be positively known until dental records have been checked.

Western Morning News

To be truly eco-friendly a coffin should be made of wicker, cardboard, papier mache, bamboo, willow or any wood from a sustainable source.

Legally a funeral can take place anywhere as long as it doesn't cause a nuisance.

From 'A Grand Exit' in Heyday magazine which carries the quote: 'My mum wants to be shot into the air with fireworks.'

Heyday magazine

An IN MEMORIAM notice for a wife and mother said: 'Always in our memory. Husband Charlie and Family. Peace at last.'

Tewkesbury Admag

Joanna Booth, the widow of a vintage shotgun expert, had her husband's ashes loaded into cartridges and used by friends for the last shoot of the season in Aberdeenshire. The cartridges were blessed by Church of Scotland minister the Rev. Alistair Donald and accounted for 70 partridges, 23 pheasants, seven ducks and one fox.

Daily Telegraph

A search for Britain's most remarkable epitaph was launched in July 2007 with this early contender:

Donald Robertson, born 14th January 1785.
Died 14th June aged 63.
He was a peaceable and quiet man, and to all appearances a sincere Christian.
His death, much regretted, was caused by the stupidity of Laurence Tulloch of Clothister (Sullom) who sold him nitre instead of Epsom Salts by which he was killed in the space of five hours.

Daily Telegraph

Award-winning novelist, playwright and columnist Keith Waterhouse – whose first job was with a firm of Leeds undertakers – recalls the days when 'somebody in our street died, the body was brought home to lie in state in the front room with all and sundry trooping through the house to pay their respects. 'Doesn't he look well?' was a common observation on these occasions.'

A few days later Mrs Heather Rubin, of Manchester, reminded Waterhouse that the inevitable rejoinder to the 'Doesn't he look well' compliment was: 'No, but he should – he's just had a week in Blackpool.'

Daily Mail

After my husband died a summons for him to do jury service arrived. I notified the court of his death and got another letter addressed to him saying: 'You have been permanently excused jury duty based on documentation indicating your permanent incapacity to serve.'

Barbara Muskin, *Reader's Digest*

A North Yorkshire man got fed up of fending off motoring fines imposed on his wife for alleged offences committed after she had died. He stormed to his local council's office carrying his wife's ashes in a casket. 'Now do you believe she's dead', he said.

Daily Mail

A car hire company in Menorca gave us a pamphlet with the following advice listed under Local Customs: 'If you see a motorcyclist raise his left hand this usually means that he is turning right. But take care as the rider may not be local, in which case he may turn left.'

Hugo Wurzer, Andover, Hampshire. *The Times*

Robert Benchley wrote an epitaph for a promiscuous actress: 'At last she sleeps alone.'

Roy Tagli, Croydon, Surrey. *Daily Telegraph*

Epitaph on a Speyside ghillie's grave in Cromdale cemetery:

'IF WHISKY BE THE
WATER OF LIFE,
THEN WHY AM I
LYING HERE?'

Kevin Melville, Fife. *Daily Telegraph*

In India, on a tombstone of a British Army officer accidentally shot by his bearer:

'WELL DONE,
THOU GOOD
AND FAITHFUL
SERVANT.'

Ray Pearce, Castle Bromwich, West Midlands.
Daily Telegraph

In the gold rush territory of Colorado there is a tombstone simply inscribed:

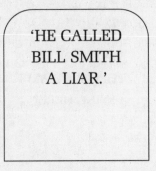

'HE CALLED
BILL SMITH
A LIAR.'

Daily Telegraph

Father Paul Nicholas, of Solihull, West Midlands, tells of visiting a parishioner in Cardiff who had been widowed. She told him her husband's ashes were in the kitchen and he expected to see an urn there. Instead, he was shown an egg timer and the widow explained: 'He never worked when he was alive, but he does now'.

Daily Telegraph

Roland Phillips, of Macclesfield, Cheshire, was amused by the funeral director's greeting card signed 'Yours eventually'.

Daily Telegraph

Jobsworth traffic wardens slapped tickets on a funeral cortege as the coffin was being carried into the hearse at Hackney, East London.

Sun

Crematorium organist Trevor Webb, of Maidstone, Kent, reports that he 'has to play too many awful things' – including travesties of 'Somewhere Over the Rainbow' and 'Danny Boy' sung by wailing pop singers. He also tells of men in shirt sleeves with their shirt tails hanging out, gum chewing and noisy chatter and laughter.

One funeral ended with a large mechanical frog being placed on the coffin.

Daily Telegraph

Two children of Annie Lamas have kept the body of their late mother on ice in a West London undertaker's cold store for ten years and visit her every week.

Independent on Sunday

Terry Prendergast, of Dorset was a World War II flying ace and when he died in May 2007, aged 85, he was buried in a coffin the shape of his beloved Hawker Hurricane – complete with cockpit, wings, propeller and the number 8608 (the number of the fighter he flew in the war).

Daily Telegraph

Ned Sherrin, 'a relentlessly mischievous and brilliant satirist', died in October 2007. When asked what he would like to be remembered for, he would say: 'Forever' (It was one of David Frost's lines that he had no hesitation in borrowing).

Daily Mail

Keith Waterhouse reported that Sherrin directed six of his plays: 'He was a ruthless script editor, removing – with the aid of a bottle of champagne – extraneous fat to produce a lean, workable play. Sometimes it was a two bottle exercise'. Keith took him a play knowing that it was too long and Sherrin said: 'I think we have a three bottle problem here, Keith'.

Daily Mail

The National Funeral Directors Association's 126th annual convention in 2007 was held in Las Vegas where they launched a 2008 calendar called Men of Mortuaries. It featured topless undertakers.

Daily Mail

Following the death in 2007 of Karlheinz Stockhausen, Paul Pastor, of Ormskirk, Lancashire wrote: 'My favourite comment on his music was by the critic who said "It's not as bad as it sounds"'.

Guardian

CHAPTER 16

TRAVEL TROUBLES

**Epitaph for a misunderstood musician:
His music was not as bad as it sounds**

Passengers were delayed for a total of 2,434 years at
Heathrow in 2006.

Daily Mail

Giles Oakley, of London, writes of a white passenger
hurling racist abuse at a black baggage handler.
Another passenger congratulated the handler for his
dignified forbearance and was told: 'That's no problem.
That passenger is flying to Berlin. His baggage is going
to Johannesburg.'

Guardian

A British railway service once famously made this excuse when snow delayed its trains: 'It was the wrong kind of snow.'

They matched this in 2007 after a French TGV train clocked up a record 357mph record with: 'Well, France is three times bigger than Britain.'

Sunday Telegraph

Joseph Rowntree (1836-1925), the Quaker philanthropist and cocoa manufacturer, once, by mistake, travelled in a first class rail coach having bought a second class ticket.

Stricken by his conscience, the next time he travelled he bought a first class ticket and travelled second class.

(Steven Burkeman, Chair, The Rowntree Society.)

Guardian

A service called MayDayCards will use their network of airline staff to carry your handwritten postcards to exotic and exclusive locations.

So, reports the *Independent on Sunday*, 'while you are staying at Mrs McGurgle's guest house in Bognor Regis, your friends think you are lounging by a pool in the Maldives.'

Independent on Sunday

Last week, at Heathrow, I saw a friend off to Nigeria. I then joined the queues of traffic to make my way to south Devon. My friend reached her destination first. Christopher Jolly of Chigwell, Essex.

Daily Telegraph

'We apologise for the lack of scenery'. Announcement on a train stuck in a tunnel in Sussex.

The Times

Excuses for late trains have become a national joke in Britain. They include autumn leaves making the tracks too slippery and trains unable to cope with 'the wrong kind of snow'. Long suffering commuters enjoyed this one from a London Underground driver: 'Your delay this evening is caused by the line controller suffering from elbow and backside syndrome – not knowing his elbow from his backside. I'll let you know any further information as soon as I am given any.'

Guardian

In 1909, the 270-mile rail trip from London to Fishguard in North Wales took four hours and 28 minutes and cost £1.75. Now it takes five hours and costs £41.

Evening Standard

In a typical city centre almost a third of the traffic consists of people driving around looking for somewhere to park.

Independent

Announcement on a railway train's public address system: 'If there is a train driver travelling on this train who knows the way to Portsmouth please could he come to the cab.'

The Times

Great moments in civil aviation. A Nepal Airlines Boeing 757, due to fly to Hong Kong, developed what appeared to be an electrical fault. Immediately two goats were taken on to the tarmac and sacrificed to appease a Hindu god. In no time at all an airline official announced: 'The snag in the plane has now been fixed and the aircraft has resumed its flight.'

Independent on Sunday

CHAPTER 17
WHAT'S IN A NAME

No bluebird has ever been seen over the White Cliffs of Dover...

George Heron, of Middlesbrough, took some clothing to the dry cleaners and was asked for his name. 'Heron,' he said. 'As in bird'.

On the ticket he was given was 'Mr Azinbird'.

Daily Telegraph

Lucinda Orr, of Charwelton, Northamptonshire, gets numerous variations on her name. Or, Oar, Ore, Ow, Hoare 'and even the less than flattering Whore.'

Daily Telegraph

The word 'verge' is French for the male organ and French visitors to Britain are delighted when they see road signs warning of Soft Verges.

Guardian

Robert Fitzgerald, of High Kelling, Norfolk, was an articled law clerk in the mid-1960s and remembers that, when his firm was acting for a property vendor called Mr Balls, a letter was written to a purchaser with the heading: 'Balls to yourself'.

A reply arrived headed: 'Balls to you too.'

The Times

The *Daily Telegraph* ran a series of letters from readers who suffer having their names spelt wrongly. No one is likely to beat the one from Tony Gyselynck, of Henley-on-Thames.

For 49 years he has been collecting the number of ways his name has been misspelt, including those on formal or official documentation.

Current score (in May 2007): 479.

Daily Telegraph

There is a firm of lawyers in Leeds called Godloves Solicitors.

Guardian

The Times diary claimed a scoop when it revealed that no bluebird has ever been seen over the white cliffs of Dover. It reveals that Vera Lynn's famous World War II song was written by an American and suggests that, perhaps, 'seagulls' simply did not scan.

The Times

Paul Surtees, of London SE25, tells *The Times* how a man barged in front of him to pay at a bookshop. The book the man was buying was entitled *Etiquette*.

The Times

There is a firm of solicitors in Leamington Spa called Wright Hassle.

Sue Holroyd, Guildford, Surrey. *Guardian*

Seen on the side of a cesspit emptiers' truck in Northamptonshire: The Motion is Carried.

Nigel Kay, Bishops Stortford, Hertfordshire.
Guardian.

Sign on a glazing repairs van in Glasgow: 'Gis a break'.

Colin Rostron, Glasgow.Guardian

Bosses are giving workers fancy titles rather than a pay rise. The *Daily Mail* reported that 'Uptitling' has become a successful way to motivate staff when budgets are tight. It suggested some examples:

- Stock Replenishment Executives (supermarket shelf stackers)
- In-Home Infant Protection Executive (baby sitter)
- Platform/Carriage Movement Facilitator (station porter)
- Technical Sanitation Assistant (lavatory cleaner)

Daily Mail

Times reader David Williams, of Leigh on Sea, Essex, spotted a Safeways' job vacancy ad for 'Ambient Replenishment'.

'I checked with a member of the staff. In plain English it means shelf stacking.'

The Times

A friend who has an evening shelf-stacking job at a supermarket tells me that, according to her contract, she is a 'Twilight Merchandiser'.

John Welford, Nuneaton, Warwickshire.
The Times

Radio 4 has a producer called Jo King and another called Will Ing.

Guardian

Children aged five are more likely to recognise Coca Cola and McDonald's logos than their own names.

Daily Telegraph

Sir Michael Caine is quoted as saying that he refuses to open any mail that is not addressed to him as 'Sir Michael'. 'I just feel that if they don't put 'Sir' on the envelope, they don't know anything about me, so why should I open the letter?'

Independent

A switchboard operator had difficulty catching my name when I wanted to leave a message for a colleague. Eventually, I said 'Noah, as in ark.' When my colleague called back he gleefully noted that the message read: 'Dr Noah Asinarc rang.'

Professor Norman Noah, *The Times*

An index of the world's most expensive signatures revealed the following prices:
The Beatles £12,500, Adolf Hitler £6,000, Winston Churchill and Marilyn Monroe £4,950.

The Times

There is a baker's shop in Glastonbury called 'Burns the Bread'.

Guardian

Beer Makers Coors discovered that its slogan 'Turn it Loose' translates into Spanish as 'Suffer from Diarrhoea'.

Reebok named a new women's tennis shoe 'Incubus'. According to medieval mythology, Incubus was a demon who ravished women in their sleep.

Coca-Cola's slogan, 'Coke Adds Life', was reportedly translated into Thai as 'Coke brings your ancestors back from the dead'.

Ford launched its Pinto in Brazil, but had to rebrand the range after it was pointed out that pinto is slang for tiny male genitals.

Guardian

Jack was the most popular boy's name in 2006. Mohammed was next (when you count up all the ones which use different spellings) and it could soon become No.1.

Daily Telegraph

Bedfordshire police have a spokesman called Lawless, Waitrose has a top executive called Mark Price, and the chief executive of the Carbon Trust is Tom Delay.

Guardian

A BBC2 current affairs programme carried an interview with a Welshman wearing a T-shirt bearing the slogan 'Twll tyn i bob Sais', which loosely translates as 'A***holes to the English'.

Daily Telegraph

The Ephraim Hardcastle column in the *Daily Mail* reports that Ed Balls, the secretary of state for schools, said that he had been teased at school about his surname, but added 'It was much worse for my sister Ophelia'.

Balls has no such sister – but Ophelia Balls flourishes up North. 'She' is a drag artist performing in the Newcastle area.

Daily Mail

All these names have been registered somewhere in the English speaking world in recent times:

- Allison Wunderland
- Dwain Pipe
- Ella Fant
- Pepperanne Salt
- Mary Chris-Smith
- Pepsi Kohler
- Polly Filler
- Russell Sprout
- Clay Potts

From *Buttering Parsnips, Twocking Chavs: The Secret Life of the English Language,* by Martin H. Manser (Orion £9.99).

Some examples from a 2007 book called *Bertha Venation and Hundreds of Other Funny Names of Real People*, by Larry Ashmead:

- Hedda Lettuce
- Stan Dupp
- Shanda Lear
- Harley Quinn

And Dwayne Dwopp must be rather tired of hearing 'Dwayne Dwopps keep falling on my head' every time he enters a room.

Daily Telegraph

Sir – Concerning funny names, David Housdon, of Elton, Cambridgeshire, recalls that when he was a lad the Rural Dean of Bedford was Canon Balls.

Daily Telegraph

The Wallasey News reports: 'A man from Love Lane pleaded guilty to a six month campaign of hate against his next-door neighbours'.

Wallasey News

A book called *Rude UK* by Rob Bailey and Ed Hurst lists 'naughty' place names and includes:
- Titup Hall Drive in Headington, Oxfordshire
- Slutshole Lane, Besthorpe, Norfolk
- Hardon Road, Wolverhampton
- Busty View, Chester-le-Street
- Slack Bottom, Heptonstall, West Yorkshire
- Bonks Hill, Sawbridgeworth, Hertfordshire
- Golden Balls Roundabout, Oxfordshire
- Husseys Lane, Hampshire
  The *Sun* says these names 'are sure to raise a smile – unless you happen to live there'.

2007 World's Worst Book Title: a children's book called *Cooking with Pooh*.

Guardian

Roger Pratt, of London EC1, says his understanding of the difference between a mechanic and an engineer is that when confronted by the same malfunction in a machine...

A mechanic would simply hit the machine with a hammer.

The engineer would think deeply on the problem, bring his expertise and experience to bear, assess the possible corrective procedures available – and then hit it with a hammer.

The Times

The BBC apologised after a radio show mentioned a plant called Black Man's Willy.

But the bloom is not alone in having a naughty name. The *Sun* exposed its readers to Knobweed, Stiffcock, Shagbark, Virgin Thistle, Nipplewort, Cockhold, Shaggy Soldier and Sticky Willy.

Sun under the headline: HARDEN OFF
YOUR KNOBWEED

In its search for the Oddest Book Title of the Year the *Bookseller* magazine came across *Tiles of the Unexpected: A Study of Six Miles of Geometric Tile Patterns on the London Underground*.

Sun

CHAPTER 18

RAISE YOUR GLASSES

Barmaid fined for crushing beer cans between her breasts...

Duncan Campbell's diary in the *Guardian* commented on all the chortling about the drinking habits of Boris Yeltsin, who died in April 2007. But, he asks, how much do our own politicians put away?

It is revealed that the House of Commons refreshment department disposed of 40,000 litres of beer, 57,300 litres of wine, and 5,700 litres of aperitifs.

'That was the consumption over 11 months,' reports Campbell. 'Pretty impressive.'

Guardian

The *Sun* pointed out that boozy Boris was merely following an age-old tradition among world leaders and gave these examples:

- William Pitt the Younger, twice British PM, was born in 1759 with gout. When he was 14 his doctor described a bottle a day of port as a cure. He took his 'medicine' throughout his life, upping the dose to three bottles a day.
- Lord George Brown, Harold Wilson's Foreign Secretary, was the man for whom the phrase 'tired and emotional' was coined. *The Times* once said: 'George Brown drunk is a better man than the Prime Minister sober.

Sun

Aileen Ashby, of London, writes: "So the government is to focus on plans to curb middle-class drinking. May I suggest alcohol-free bars at the Palace of Westminster?"

The Times

There are some 460 words for 'drunk' in Bob Holder's dictionary *How Not To Say What You Mean*. They include: blotto, boiled, half-stewed, legless, loaded, plastered, wired, zonked, Brahms, half-foxed, chemically inconvenienced and p****d.

Sun

George Melly, described in The Times as a louche, lecherous and lovable jazzman and the British equivalent of a Turkish belly dancer, died in July 2007 aged 80. He wore florid zoot suits and fedora hats and was once an 80-a-day smoker. He also claimed to have drunk a bottle of brandy every night, on top of wine and gin during the day. In later life he claimed to have cut down to 'almost teetotalism' – consuming in a day only a dry sherry, several gins, a couple of brandies and an unspecified amount of wine – a degree of moderation that would fell an ox.

Melly's wit was legendary. He once asked Mick Jagger why his face was so wrinkled. Jagger said the wrinkles were laughter lines.

Melly quipped: 'Nothing's that funny.'

The Times / Guardian

Hertfordshire student Jack Kirby drank the contents of 4,000 Budweiser cans and built a life-sized model of a 1965 Ford Mustang with the empties.

Independent on Sunday

Scotland tops the world UFO league with 300 sightings a year – but drink is not to blame, say experts.

Independent on Sunday

When it's closing time on Friday nights in the pubs of Kensington, the landlord shouts: 'Come on, haven't you got second homes to go to?'

John O'Farrell, *Guardian*

Scientists have discovered that people look more attractive after a couple of drinks. Experiments show that what is known in the trade as the 'beer goggle effect' actually does exist.

Sunday Times

When the ban on smoking in public places began in 2007 a pub in Pickering in North Yorkshire put up this notice:

A WARM WELCOME TO ALL
WARNING: STAFF MAY BECOME STROPPY
OR VIOLENT DUE TO LACK OF
PASSIVE SMOKING.

Daily Mail

Always carry a large flagon of whisky in case of snakebite, and furthermore always carry a small snake.

W. C. Fields quoted in *The Little Book of Whisky Tips*

Bawdy limericks were common forms of entertainment in the English taverns of the 15th and 16th centuries. Paul Vallely enjoyed a two-page romp on them in the Independent, and among the gems he came up with was 'a rather rude one':

There was a young woman from Leeds
Who swallowed a packet of seeds
Within half an hour
Her tits were in flower
And her fanny was covered in weeds

Another one came from former Prime Minister Clement Attlee who wrote about himself:

Few thought he was even a starter
There were many in life who were smarter
But he finished PM
A CH and OM
An earl and Knight of the Garter

Independent

An Australian barmaid was fined for crushing beer cans between her breasts – in breach of hotel licensing laws.

Sunday Times

Peter Dolan left his carthorse Peggy outside the Alexandra hotel in Jarrow, South Tyneside. But the rope was too long and Peggy followed him into the bar and was given a pint of John Smiths. She is now a regular – and is also partial to pickled onion crisps.

The Times

The Queen Mother's longevity has been put down to 'industrial quantities of gin, champagne and claret. They appear to have been her recipe for long life', says a Guardian review of *Behind Closed Doors* by former equerry Colin Burgess (published by John Blake).

At dinner parties, 'if she felt the ice needed to be broken, she would lob a cork or a roll at someone and shout 'Catch that'. In the last ten years of her life (she died aged 101) 'you got the impression that she felt, 'Wow, I'm still here, let's enjoy it'.

Guardian

Oddd pub sign in Carlton village, East Yorkshire, spotted by Mrs S. Walmsley, of Rochdale, Lancashire:

THE ODDDFELLOWS ARMS

Had the signwriter had one too many? asks Mrs Walmsley.
Daily Mail

I was recently stopped while driving at 39mph in a 40mph zone. 'Nobody does that at 2.00am unless he has been drinking', said the policeman. After a negative breath test I was asked why I had been travelling below the speed limit. 'Because,' I said, 'there was a police car behind me'.

Alan Calvered, Bishop's Stortford. *Independent*

When builder Neil Irwin goes out drinking he wears a T-shirt bearing his address and a photograph of his house so folk can see him home in Herne Bay, Kent.

Sun

Soon after it became illegal to smoke in public places pub customers grew nostalgic for the old familiar smells. A Lancashire firm specialising in 'niche fragrances' started getting orders for an 'ashtray aerosol scent' which recreates the authentic fug of a pub.

Independent on Sunday

The Old Spot Inn in Dursley, Gloucestershire, won the 2008 Pub of the Year Award from the Campaign for Real Ale. There is no juke box, no pool table, no fruit machine – and it doesn't serve chips. Licensee Steve Herbert says: 'Our drinkers come first'.

The Times

This is stuff we all need to know. Michael Winner, lover of expensive wines, says: 'If you buy a Chateau Latour 1961 in a restaurant, probably for £8,000 a bottle, it is opened and poured immediately. So, allowing for three hours breathing, your Latour would be just about ready to drink as you get up to leave. I get round this problem when I take my own wines by pouring them out at home into a decanter and let them breathe away to their hearts' content in my living room. Sometimes I pour my wine from the decanter into a milk bottle and take this to the restaurant. Amazingly, the lady accompanying me refuses to carry the milk bottles. She thinks it looks terrible. But what do I care if I'm saving a couple of thousand pounds on restaurant prices?'

Daily Mail

A new pub called The John Masefield in New Ferry, the Wirral, has been urged to change its sign because its image of the former Poet Laureate looks more like Hitler. Locals began calling the inn The Adolf and the *Sun*'s headline was ALE HITLER. It also suggested ONE FUHRER THE ROAD and HERR OF THE DOG.

Sun

The campaign to crack down on binge drinking ran into difficulties when it was reported that anti-binge drinking adverts were not working. Ads warning of the dangers of booze often show people passing out or being carried home. But researchers found that these scenes could remind youngsters of fun nights out and a Bath University professor said that young people bonded over tales of alcohol-fuelled disasters.

Sun

New sex discrimination laws mean that landlords could be punished for allowing sexist jokes in their pubs. Defiantly the *Daily Mail* filled a page with jokes that would fall foul of the new legislation:

- A horse walks into a bar and asks the barmaid for a drink. 'Why the long face?' asks the barmaid.
- A penguin walks into a bar and asks the barmaid: 'Have you seen my brother?' 'I don't know,' she replies. 'What does he look like?'
- A giraffe walks into a bar and orders a pint and is charged £10. The barmaid says: 'We don't get many giraffes in here.' 'At your prices I'm not surprised,' says the giraffe.

Daily Mail

CHAPTER 19
SCHOOL'S OUT

**Jilly has set herself an
extremely low standard which she
has failed to maintain...**

University lectures are increasingly being moved to
the afternoons to give students more time in bed.

Daily Telegraph

**Charles Wilkie-Smith, of Corbridge, Northumberland
recalled his final prep school history report which said:
'Charles Smith slept here.'**

The Times

Andy Du Port, of Chichester, West Sussex, was
taught rowing and geography by the same master
and got a school report which said: 'Good at rivers'.

The Times

An exasperated colleague wrote on one pupil's school report: 'John is to design technology what Attila the Hun was to needlework.'

Henry Adams, Wirral, Merseyside. *The Times*

In the 1960s I was told that the only words required in school reports were: 'Trying' and 'Very'.

Jean Bryant, East Grinstead, West Sussex.
The Times

Arnold Freedman treasures his school report saying: 'Should have done well, but has fallen into bad company.' In a letter to *The Times* he reports: 'I became a consultant surgeon. The bad company became a professor of physics.'

The Times

School report on the son of a professor of mathematics: 'Not up to pa.'

Robert Hudson, Warwick. *The Times*

A report from the Latymer Upper School, Hammersmith: 'We have both failed. I, at least, tried'.

Kenneth Cleveland, Carlisle. *The Times*

A head teacher remembers this report: 'I have spent more time on X's homework than he has.'
David Porter, Bury St. Edmunds, Suffolk.

The Times

Lee Jones of Manchester got a note from school complaining about 'incomplete and poorly attempted' homework. He admitted that he had not submitted homework for a some time, but pointed out that he is now approaching his 21st birthday and left school four years ago.

Sun

A schoolboy was asked 'Who was Joan of Arc' and he replied: 'Noah's wife.'
Mrs Elizabeth Price, Linton, Kent.

Daily Mail

Geography Awareness Week 2007 had a survey asking: 'Where is Mount Everest?' One in three thought it was in the Alps – or tucked away somewhere in Britain.

Daily Mail

From a school report on novelist Jilly Cooper: 'Jilly has set herself an extremely low standard which she has failed to maintain'.

Daily Mail

Organisers of TV quiz shows, aware of the limitations of many of the people leaving school these days, often make it easier with multiple choice questions. Andrew Pierce, in his *Daily Telegraph* Notebook, writes: 'Can I share this gem from the Big Brother house? A beauty queen was asked if Winston Churchill was:

- A rapper
- A US president
- A prime minister
- A king

The 21-year-old contestant replied: 'Wasn't he the first black president of America? There's a statue of him near me that's black'.

Daily Telegraph

One in three children think Winston Churchill was the first man on the moon, according to a survey. Four in ten thought Mars was only a choc bar.

Sun

A fifth of British teenagers believe Sir Winston Churchill was a fictional character, while many think Sherlock Holmes and Eleanor Rigby were real.

Daily Telegraph

On ITV's *This Morning* programme the quizmaster asked a contestant: 'On which river is Newcastle situated?'

Contestant: 'The Thames'.

Quizmaster: 'Yes, well done!'

Daily Mail (selecting extracts from *Mediaballs,* edited by Marcus Berkmann).

The British may well express pride in the nation's heritage, but lots of them are ignorant about it. A survey found:

- 1 in 10 adults thought Hitler was not a real person and almost half were convinced that Robin Hood was.
- More than half thought Horatio Nelson commanded British troops at the battle of Waterloo.
- 30% of 11 to 18 year olds thought that Oliver Cromwell fought at the Battle of Hastings.

'In a way,' sighed an expert, 'there is just too much history.'

Sunday Telegraph

James Meadows, of London, says his school motto was 'Age Quod Agis' (do as you would be done by), which 'we chose to translate as "Do it to him before he does it to you."'

Guardian

Derek Craven, of Bath, says that in 1940 his class motto was 'Cras Fortasse Laborabimus' – tomorrow, perhaps, we shall work.

Daily Telegraph

TV and radio quiz shows are now some of the funniest programmes thanks to stupid answers given by many contestants. For instance:

Q: Name the funny men who once entertained kings and queens at court.
A: Lepers

Q: A famous chain of tea shops was opened in London in 1894 by Joseph who?
A: Goebbels

Q: Name someone associated with Liverpool.
A: My uncle Peter.

From *Private Eye's Dumb Britain*, edited by Marcus Berkmann £4.99. *Daily Mail*

New Government guidance in April 2007 told teachers that unruly pupils should not be 'overdisciplined'. Teachers should hand out praise five times more often than punishments.

This inspired cartoonist Haldane to show a teacher telling a miscreant to 'Go to the headmaster's office for tea and biscuits'.

The Times

In May 2007 Education Secretary Alan Johnson told the House of Commons how he had been caned by a teacher called Hughes in 1959.

In the *Daily Mail* of 8 June 2007 a Mr David Hughes, a retired teacher of Bury St Edmunds, Suffolk, stated that he was not the teacher who caned Johnson, but 'when I listen to him now I would be greatly tempted to.'

Daily Mail

Henry Smith, of Hove, East Sussex, remembers the motto of the Brighton, Hove and Sussex Grammar School: 'Absque Labore Nihil' (Without Labour Nothing).

Much amusement was caused when the building became Brighton's Maternity Hospital and the motto remained on the façade.

Daily Telegraph

Keith Waterhouse likes the motto of Penistone Grammar School: 'Learn or Leave'.

Daily Mail

David Cowling, of Perth, says his school's motto was 'something about Gloria being sick in a Transit'.

Guardian

Dudley Turner, of Westerham, Kent, pointed out that Gloria was sick only on a Mundi.

Guardian

In July 2007 the Scouts celebrated 100 years of the movement. It may have begun as an adventure club with proficiency badges in stopping runaway horses and bugling, but today's scouts pick up qualifications in administration or public relations or circus skills. Rosie Reynolds, 16, from Eltham, South London, said: 'I do not know how to tie any sort of knot.'

Guardian

Does nothing change? 'In 1912 *The Times* quoted a headmaster saying that standards of reading were declining because parents no longer read to their children – and too much time was spent listening to the gramophone'.

Alan Myers, Hitchin, Hertfordshire. *Sunday Times*

I was asked by a pupil if it is true that, on reaching the age of 100, one receives a mammogram from the Queen.

Ron Sloggett, of Fleet, Hampshire. *Daily Telegraph*

Oxbridge has become famous for throwing oddball questions into interviews with students. (Such as: 'Tell me about a banana'.) But gone are the days of the Cambridge tutor who was said to hurl a rugby ball at interviewees. If they dropped it they were out. If they caught it they were in. If they drop-kicked it through the window they got a scholarship.

Daily Telegraph

There was a time when the essential skills acquired by a Girl Guide included semaphore, making beds and lighting fires. However, a 2007 *Guide to Living For Modern Girls* says that the must-have skills for 7-10 year olds should include surfing the web safely and being able to name the Prime Minister.

10-15 year olds should be able to stand up to boys, change a light bulb and know self defence.

At 16 to 25 they should know how to practise safe sex, speak confidently in public, cook a roast dinner and keep down their carbon footprints.

Daily Telegraph

Ten things every girl should know:
- How to knit
- Basic Ballet
- Bake cupcakes
- Make a daisy chain
- How to eat spaghetti
- The perfect French plait
- Grow cress from seed
- Climb a tree
- Sew on a button
- Play conkers

The Times

Brighton College plans to teach traditional etiquette to its pupils. The news inspired John Venning, Head of English at St Paul's, London SW13, to write of an encounter with one of his senior pupils. 'If this encounter had occurred 50 years ago, the boy might have "capped" me as he passed. Instead he removed the earphone of his MP3 player, said "Good morning, sir", and returned the earphone to his ear'.

Daily Telegraph

A teacher told a pupil that it was impossible for a whale to swallow a human being and the pupil said: 'When I get to Heaven I will ask Jonah'. 'What if Jonah went to hell?', asked the teacher. 'Then you can ask him', said the pupil.

Daily Mail

Consultants were paid £5,000 to find a name for a new university at Bradford. They came up with: 'Bradford University, University of Bradford and The University of Bradford'.

Telegraph and Argus

CHAPTER 20

PLAIN ECCENTRIC

**While clearing the house of
a deceased aunt, a box was discovered,
labelled, correctly: 'Pieces of string
too short to keep.'**

A book with the title *Fish Who Answer the
Telephone and Other Bizarre Books* (by Russell Ash
and Brian Lake, published by John Murray £9.99)
includes: *Eleven Years as a Drunkard, or, The Life
of Thomas Doner, Having Lost Both Arms Through
Intemperance, He Wrote This Book With His Teeth
as a Warning to Others.*

Reader's Digest

A long established British eccentricity is love of
queuing. *Reader's Digest* reports on research showing
that Britons spend 407 hours a year shopping – 73 of
those hours being spent in queues.

Reader's Digest

In 1984 a notice began appearing in Edinburgh newspapers asking: 'Are you eccentric or know someone who may be?' Among the results:

- The Barking Vicar of Berkshire, whose sermons featured animal growls.
- An inventor who created a tripod on which country singer Dolly Parton could rest her breasts.
- A Yorkshireman who lectured sheep from a pulpit atop his farmhouse.
- Anne Atkins, who had more than 1,000 garden gnomes in her Gnome Reserve. She accepted visitors if they wore the tall, red gnome hats which she provided. 'Otherwise, the gnomes are embarrassed by people staring at them. This way, the gnomes think the visitors are just other, larger gnomes.'

Wall Street Journal

Mike Madden, 48, went walking in the woods near Huddersfield, West Yorkshire, wearing a bird-feeding hat complete with a tray full of nuts. From the top of a tree, a large grey squirrel took a flying leap at Mr Madden's hat. The impact knocked the bird lover to the ground and he suffered whiplash injuries requiring him to wear a neck brace for a week. Mr Madden calls himself an inventor and gives his address as Crackpot Cottage.

The Times

The e-petitions received on No.10's website reveal some of the oddball things that excite the interest of the Great British Public. They include calls for:

- Legislation to introduce a standard-sized umbrella.
- Spandau Ballet's song Gold to be the new national anthem
- Yorkshire pudding to become the internationally recognised symbol of the North of England.
- A Bank Holiday in memory of the world's oldest horse (Old Billy, which died in 1822 aged at least 62).
- Frisbee to become an Olympic sport.

No.10 does reject some petitions. One was a plea for mice to be allowed to travel free on public transport – rejected not because it was deemed frivolous, but because it was 'outside the remit or powers of the Prime Minister'.

The Times

Sixty-nine year-old Peter Taylor of Hastings, East Sussex, writes in the *Daily Telegraph*: 'I drive an MGF 1.81 convertible Rover. When the hood is down I wear a felt hat with one side turned up and the flap garnished with seagull and flamingo feathers mixed with sprigs from a long-stemmed decorative flower'.

Daily Telegraph

72-year-old Betty Rees of Solihull, West Midlands, drove an ancient Ford Fiesta and bought her clothes in charity shops. She left £1.2million to animal charities in her will – some of it for donkeys in Egypt.

Daily Mail

A baked bean fanatic who calls himself Capt Beany and paints himself orange has been declared an official tourist attraction in Port Talbot South Wales.

South Wales Evening Post

Joseph Leek of Hull wore second hand clothes, lived in a dilapidated house and watched his neighbour's TV to save money on electricity. When he died at the age of 90 he left £1.1 million to the Guide Dogs for the Blind Association – a charity in which he had never shown any interest. He left his two daughters nothing.

The Times

A four-page leaflet has been published in Dundee giving advice on the safest way to sit on the toilet. It is entitled Good Defecation Dynamics.

From Richard Littlejohn's book, *Littlejohn's Britain* (Hutchinson £12.99). *Daily Mail*

A letter in *The Times* read simply: 'Sir, While clearing the house of a deceased aunt we found a box labelled, correctly: "Pieces of string too short to keep"'.

This was followed by a spate of similar letters, including:

'Years ago, after the death of my husband's great aunt, I found a tin labelled: "Old toffees. Not to be eaten"'.

'We found a parcel, labelled in my great grandmother's handwriting: "Old blanket. Too good for cow"'.

'Soon after my grandmother's death we were much amused to find among the odds and ends a bottled labelled "Might Be Aspirin"'. Jean Gibbs, Sidmouth, Devon.

The Times

Eccentric millionaire Sir Owen Aisher died aged 93 in 1993. He was the chairman of Marley Tiles and produced a range of new floorings – and the first British hula-hoops. In later life he amused himself by shooting trout from his electric wheelchair.

Daily Mail

Sir George Sitwell, father of Dame Edith, invented a small revolver specifically for shooting wasps. He used it with some success in company.

Ronald Hampton, Horncastle, Lincs.

Daily Telegraph

Sir George was an example of English eccentricity at its finest. He also invented a musical toothbrush which played Annie Laurie and had a notice at his home, Renishaw Hall, Derbyshire, which said: 'I must ask anyone entering the house never to contradict me in anyway as it interferes with the functioning of the gastric juices and prevents my sleeping at night'.

The Age

Simon Boyd-Wallis, of Petersfield, West Sussex followed up the Sitwell wasp shooting story saying that unbeknown to most people, the wasp-shooting season starts in earnest in the summer. This exacting sport requires a .177 air pistol. A target is smeared with jam and highest points are scored only when the wasp ambles over the centre.

Daily Telegraph

CHAPTER 21

A TOUCH OF CLASS

Man called Pratt kicked out of gentleman's club – for being a prat...

The class system is still alive in Britain. A 2008 survey recorded 88% saying so.

The Times

Sir Charles Clore once said: 'We should all be happy with what we have.' He was sitting in the back of his Rolls Corniche.

Maurice Cross, of Bristol, in the *Daily Mail*

'I would never go out with a man who, when boarding an aircraft, turned right'.

Tara Palmer-Tomkinson. *Sunday Times*

The most immediately striking fact in the recent obituary of Lord Michael Pratt is that he was once kicked out of Pratt's (the 150 year-old gentleman's club) for being a prat.

In what must be the least hagiographic obit ever published in the *Telegraph*, Michael John Henry Pratt, youngest son of the fifth Marquess of Camden, is summed up as an 'unabashed snob and interloper on a grand scale'. (Hagiography is the study of saints.)

Guardian

A fine example of post code snobbery. A letter in the *Daily Telegraph* tells of a cleaning company writing to a woman with a posh post code suggesting she took on a regular and reliable cleaner.

Her daughter had a less posh post code and got a letter from the same company saying that there was plenty of regular and reliable work available... As a cleaner.

Daily Telegraph

Sue MacGregor, a BBC presenter whose cool professionalism has made her a national institution, tells in her memoirs how colleague Sandra Harrison asked Dame Barbara Cartland if she thought that, in modern Britain, class doesn't matter any more. 'Of course it doesn't, darling,' came the answer, 'or I wouldn't be talking to you!'

Daily Mail

The *Washington Post*'s London bureau chief was invited to tea at 10 Downing Street. When he asked: 'What time is teatime?' he was told: 'It depends what class you are. It's about 4pm, with cucumber sandwiches, for some, and 6pm for those who want pie and chips'.

Observer

'The class divisions in this country can easily be distinguished. The lower classes drop litter, the middle classes don't and the upper classes pick up the lower classes' litter.'

S. G. Davies in the *Daily Telegraph*

If you have your name on your overalls you are working class. If your name is on your desk you are middle class. If it is on the factory you are upper-class.

Pete Stephenson, Buxton, Derbyshire. *Guardian*

Sociologists state that the middle classes are defined by their behaviour. I found my nine-year-old daughter soaking her conkers in balsamic vinegar.

John Duckworth, Hampton Court. *The Times*

A true gentleman is never rude unintentionally.

The Times

BARMY BRITAIN

The editor of *Debrett's Peerage*, Zoe Gullen, says that the point about etiquette is that it should reflect good manners and is not inflexible. She cites the occasion when the Queen saw a guest drinking from his finger bowl – and followed suit.

Daily Mail

Following a proposal that it might be a good idea if people living in 'nice areas' paid more council tax than those living in 'rough areas', a critic complained that his neighbours were an extended family run by a woman with a pack of dogs. 'Her car isn't taxed or insured and doesn't have a number plate. Her grumpy old man is famous for upsetting foreigners with racist comments. A local shopkeeper claims the grumpy old man ordered the murder of his son's girlfriend. Two of the kids have broken marriages and two grandsons are meant to be in the Army, but are always in night clubs. The family's antics are forever in the papers. They're out of control. Who'd want to live near Windsor Castle?'

Sunday Telegraph

Edward Bryant, of Paris, said: 'Every elegant dresser knows that the tie should not be the same colour as the shirt or the suit'.

Daily Telegraph

C. J. G. Macy of Lincoln pointed out that it costs £5 or more to have a pocket added to a shirt. Have the upper classes abandoned them because they can't afford them?

Daily Telegraph

Should men's shirts have breast pockets? Controversy raged in the newspapers during November 2007. 'Snobs have got it in for shirt pockets', said a *Daily Telegraph* article, printing the argument that 'A gentleman needs no tools, so why should he need a pocket?' Chris Watson, of Perak, Malaysia, said that a worse crime is surely a tie with a short-sleeve shirt.

Daily Telegraph

CHAPTER 22
COUNCIL DAZE

**Driver throws his parking ticket
down in disgust and gets another ticket
for causing litter...**

A Hertford traffic warden slapped a ticket on her own vehicle after it was pointed out that her permit was out of date.

Daily Telegraph

A Twickenham shopkeeper sounds a World War II air raid siren when a traffic warden is sighted in his road.

Independent on Sunday

The workers who sweep England's roads have always been known as road-sweepers. But in an extreme example of political correctness, Liverpool city council now calls them 'Street Scene Operatives'.

Daily Mail

Residents of the remote village of East Prawle in Devon found that the only way they could get their mobiles to work was to stand on a bench on the village green and face west.

Queues began to snake back from the bench at peak times and it began to show signs of wear and tear. So the parish council decided to build them a podium.

Guardian

April 2007 was marked with bitter controversy over some councils deciding to empty dustbins once a fortnight instead of once a week.

It all reminded Rodney Morgan-Giles, of Alresford, Hampshire, of an Osbert Lancaster cartoon during the dustmen's strike in the 1970s. It had a civil servant saying: 'We don't have a problem. We file all our rubbish.'

Daily Telegraph

Councillor Chris Lewis got a parking ticket – while carrying out a survey on car parking in Paignton, Devon. He was checking for places which might be suitable for parking meters – and left his Jeep in a taxi bay.

Sun

Aimee Green did not have any change when she parked in Coulsdon, Surrey, so she put £1 in the meter instead of 80p. She was astonished when she returned 15 minutes later to find a traffic warden giving her a ticket because she 'had paid for more time than was allowed'. The local council cancelled the £60 penalty notice and said that the jobsworth warden 'had been spoken to.'

Evening Standard

Blacksmith Robert McFarland left his horse in the street and returned to find that a traffic warden had slapped a parking ticket on it – with the words 'brown horse' under the vehicle description.

It is one of the barmy incidents in *The Parking Ticket Awards* book by Barrie Segal (Portico Books £6.99), who runs a website fighting unlawful tickets. The book also includes:

- A truck getting a ticket while stuck in a huge hole after a road collapsed.
- A hearse getting a ticket while undertakers were loading a coffin on to it.
- An abandoned burnt out car with no tyres or windscreen. It got three tickets.

News of the World

A builder got fed up with getting parking tickets outside a property he was renovating. So he hired a skip with a drop down front and parked it outside the property. Every day he drove his van into the skip – and the parking tickets stopped.

From *The Parking Ticket Awards* by Barry Segal, published by Portico £6.99. *Daily Mail*

Segal's book also tells of a delivery driver who threw his parking ticket down in disgust – and was fined by a warden on litter patrol.

Daily Mail

A member of South Staffordshire District Council spent £2,300 of his official allowance on a speed camera for his ward. He became one of its first victims – caught doing 43mph in a 30mph zone. The policeman who flagged him down was reported to have 'had difficulty in hiding a smile.'

Daily Telegraph

In an attempt to drive away rough sleepers from a multi-storey car park, Stoke on Trent council arranged for Beethoven's Symphony No.9 in D minor to be played continuously.

Guardian

Council workers who turned up to mend a broken window at the home of a disabled woman in the West Midlands replaced every window in the house except the broken one.

Guardian

If you clear snow from the pavement outside your home you could be liable if someone slips on it. If you leave the snow alone the council would be liable.

The Times

'Not only do the homeless not have anywhere to play badminton or tennis, they don't have anywhere to live either.'

Councillor Arthur Mandry, quoted in the
Fareham Journal

Only one member of the public turned up for a discussion organised by Bath and North East Somerset Council to find ways of combating voter apathy.

Bristol Evening Post

A report advising Rotherham council how to be efficient and save money has had to be redrafted 12 times. Total cost £12,000.

Sheffield Star

Two motorists parked in a road in Islington, London, N1, where yellow no parking lines had been erased by roadworks. Later yellow lines were painted underneath the vehicles and ten minutes later they were clamped. A council spokesman said: 'It was a daft mistake. We apologise.'

Sun

Light bulb changing can be a formidable task. Doncaster Council's community care staff are alerted to health and safety rules and electrical safety legislation. These regulations require a second person to hold any ladder being used by the person changing the bulb. A third person is needed to switch off the electricity at the mains and stay by the switch until the bulb is changed. Where the client is frail or anxious there may be the need of a fourth person to comfort them while the operation is completed. Many home care workers are not allowed to change light bulbs.

Guardian

It can cost £50 and involve five people working in three different buildings to get a Hull Council light bulb changed. The *Daily Mail* outlined the procedure:

Step 1:   Report broken light to superintendent's office.

Step 2:   Superintendent faxes Property Services.

Step 3:   Property Services issues order for new bulb to Works Department.

Step 4:   Works Department issues job sheet to electrician.

Step 5:   Electrician fits bulb.

The procedure can take up to five weeks.

Daily Mail

CHAPTER 23

LET US PRAY

Church 'Healing Service' cancelled
due to illness...

It may not result in you breaking into uncontrolled laughter, but in 1993 the *Independent* carried a report on 'A Theory of Humour Elicitation'.

The complex report was softened by opening with a joke about a priest who was accosted by a prostitute offering a quickie for £20.

The priest ignores her but is later approached by another prostitute making the same offer.

Arriving at the seminary the priest asks a nun: 'What's a quickie?'

And the nun says: '£20, same as in town'.

Independent

Broadcaster and author John Humphrys' new book is entitled *In God We Doubt*, and it reminded Simon Hoggart of this joke.

A man anxiously seeking a parking space prays to God, saying he will give up drink, smoking and sex if he can find one. One immediately appears and the driver looks up to tell God: 'It's all right, I've found one.'

Guardian

A local church's wild flower meadow in Torquay boasted a luxuriance of agrimony, betony, birdsfoot, trefoil, cowslip, greater knapweed and devils-bit scabious. But the town's maintenance department sent in a man on a sit-on mower. He razed the carefully cultivated plot which had been financed by their own council. It had all looked 'rather unkempt', they said.

The Friends of the Churchyard fumed: 'Looking wild was rather the point. It's a typical case of the left hand not knowing what the right hand's doing at the council.'

The Times

A Healing Service at Acton Church had to be cancelled due to illness.

From Mr. Manning, Acton, Suffolk. *Daily Mail*

It could have come straight from Carry on Campanology: a bell ringer tugs on a rope and promptly disappears up into the belfry. But it was no joke for 14-year-old James Kemp when a stay that stops the bells swinging snapped at St John the Baptist Church in Loughton, Essex. James's rope shot upwards and he went 15ft up with it.

James said: 'I went up so fast I didn't realise until my hand hit the ceiling – that's when I let go.'

James was fortunate not to break any bones and his mother said: 'It hasn't put him off. All hobbies can be dangerous – even bell ringing I suppose.'

Metro

The Methodist Church launched a competition to find an 11th Commandment. Among suggestions were 'Never give out your password'. Political philosopher Roger Scruton came up with: 'Thou shalt not think of any more Commandments.' The *Sunday Telegraph*'s report ended with: 'For many modern sinners the traditional 11th Commandment 'Thou shalt not get found out' will take some beating.'

The winner of the competition was 'Thou shall not be negative'. Runners up included: 'Thou shall not worship false pop idols' and 'Thou shalt not consume thine own bodyweight in fudge.'

The Times

Norman Sanders from Ipswich asked: 'Was it not Bertrand Russell who said that the Commandments should be treated like an examination – only six need be attempted?'

The Times

Churchgoers in the Cotswolds are reminded that not everybody enjoys baked beans as much as the British and are asked to not to bring them as harvest festival offerings.

Guardian

As a child in Kent, the lack of punctuation on the church collection box filled me with wonder and awe: 'Thanks Be To God This Box Is Emptied Daily.'

Gillian Bailey, London SW4. *Independent*

The Bishop of Horsham urged Sussex vicars to take horse dung into their services to make the Nativity more realistic.

Daily Mirror

A parrot took up residence in the bell tower of St Mary's church at Mirfield, West Yorkshire, and started telling worshippers to 'f*** off'. The vicar said: 'Most people find it funny, but it can cause problems at funerals'.

Sunday Times

Would the congregation please note that the bowl at the back of the church labelled 'for the sick' is for monetary donations only.

Churchtown Parish Magazine

An ongoing debate comparing the Bible with the IKEA catalogue produced this letter from John O'Byrne, of Harold's Cross, Dublin: 'Nowhere in the Old Testament is there a mention of God creating the world in six days and on the seventh finding a whole solar system left over.'

The Times

Emporer Menelik II of Ethiopia is said to have eaten pages of the Bible whenever he felt unwell. Following a stroke in 1913 he devoured the entire Book of Kings and subsequently died of an intestinal obstruction.
Roger De B. Hovell, Pangbourne, Berks. *Daily Telegraph*

'We shall be meeting on Wednesday when the subject will be 'Heaven. How do we get there?' Transport is available at 7.55pm from the bus stop opposite the Harewood Arms.'

The magazine of the parish of
Collingham-with-Harewood

We are pleased to announce the birth of David Anthony Brown, the only sin of the Rev and Mrs J. B. Brown.
The Ambleside Methodist Newsletter

A notice on the edge of the large fish and water lily pool at the Royal Army Chaplains' Department Centre, Bagshot Park, Surrey read: 'Please do not walk on the water'.

The Times

Worshippers in East Sussex are told that, due to Health and Safety regulations, fresh produce is no longer welcome at harvest festivals. They are asked to bring tinned food, cook-in sauces, biscuits, jam and custard powder.

The Times

When we were children my brother asked my father if it was right that we come from dust and return to dust. Father said yes and my brother said: 'There is someone coming or going under my bed.'
S. Hobson, Croydon, Surrey.

Daily Mail

In the midst of the fierce debate about whether it should be made illegal to tell jokes about ethnic minorities and their religions, it still seems to be fair game for the British to poke fun at each other. M. G. Bowman, of Fordingbridge, Hampshire, recalls some golden oldies in the *Daily Telegraph*:

- The English regard themselves as a self-made nation, which relieves the Almighty of a terrible responsibility.
- The Scots keep the Sabbath – and anything else they can lay their hands on.
- The Welsh pray on their knees and on their neighbours.
- The Irish don't know what they want, but will fight for it anyway.

Daily Telegraph

Julie Langdon's Notebook recalled the time when a former Archbishop of Canterbury disembarked in New York from a transatlantic liner. He was asked by an impudent American reporter if he was planning to visit any nightclubs in New York.

'Are there any nightclubs in New York?' the Archbishop responded, innocently.

The headline next morning was: 'Archbishop's First Question: Are there any nightclubs in New York?'

Daily Telegraph

British Servicemen imprisoned by the Japanese sought some little solace in cigarettes which they had to make themselves.

Bible pages were ideal for this purpose and they asked their chaplain for permission to use them.

Permission was given with the provision that they read every word on the pages first.

Rev. Dr A. A. Macintosh, Cambridge.

Daily Telegraph

CHAPTER 24

MIND YOUR LANGUAGE

**The fear of long words is called
Hippopotomonstrosesquippedaliophobia...**

Beijing has been busy correcting more than 6,500 traffic signs in a bid to eradicate bad English before the 2008 Olympics.

Its Ethnic Minorities Park was originally signposted 'Racist Park'.

Sunday Times

Alan Norris, of Loughton, Essex, asked a Tesco supermarket assistant where he could find cloves and was told only their larger stores sold 'cloves'.

The Times

There was controversy over British sailors being allowed to sell their stories after being seized and held by Iran.

When pressed in the Commons to apologise, Defence Secretary Des Browne used the phrase: 'I have expressed a degree of regret that can be equated with an apology.'

The *Observer* commented: 'We were highly impressed by his nimble manipulation of the English language. Still, you do wonder if, sometimes, it might not be easier to say sorry.'

Observer

A *Daily Mail* reader wrote in about that sentence which uses the word 'had' ten times in a row ('James while John had had had had had had had had had had had a better effect on the teacher') and came up with one which has 13 'ands' in a row.

'When a company called Holland and Andrews had a new sign painted, the sign writer got the spacing wrong.

'The company complained: "There is too much space between Holl and and and and and and and And and And and And and drews."'
Rick Legend, Cyprus.

Daily Mail

In a BBC search for the worst ever pop lyric Des'ree's song 'Life' got the 'honour' with:

> *I don't want to see a ghost*
> *It's the sight that I fear most*
> *I'd rather have a piece of toast.*

Despite a late run there was no place in the top ten for Shakira's 'Whenever, Wherever':

> *Lucky that my breasts are small and humble*
> *So you don't confuse them with the mountains.*

The Times

Adam Jacob de Boinod has produced two compendiums of unlikely, but useful, words that other languages enjoy but English does not. They include:

- **Baku-shan (Japanese)** – a woman who looks better from behind.
- **Nakhur (Farsi)** – a camel that won't give milk until its nostrils are tickled.
- **Tantenverfuhrer (German)** – an aunt seducer.
- **Pesamentiero (Portugese)** – one who habitually joins mourners at the homes of the deceased to get at the free refreshments.
- **Chapponner (Gallo dialect of French)** – sticking a finger up a chicken's bottom to see if it is about to lay an egg.

The Times

The fear of long words is called
Hippopotomonstrosesquippedaliophobia.

Reader's Digest

My late grandfather used to tell me that while there were only 36 words in English containing the letters 'ough' there were nine different ways of pronouncing them - all of which could be found in the rather obscure sentence: 'Though a rough cough and hiccoughs ploughed through him, he houghed the horse with thorough thoughtfulness'. Nicholas Pritchard, Southampton.

The Times

Having breakfast at Heathrow Airport, I asked the waitress whether the orange juice was freshly squeezed and she replied: 'It's freshly squeezed out of a carton.' English is indeed a wonderfully rich language.

Matthew Dick, West Sussex. *The Times*

The stormtroopers of the Equal Opportunities Commission never sleep. A journalist filming a stand at the Commission's conference asked if the stand was manned. 'It is never manned', was the frosty response. 'It is staffed'.

Daily Mirror

A language kit designed to help British long-distance lorry drivers criss-crossing the linguistic frontiers of Europe enables them to order chips in six languages.

The Times

Luigi Amaduzzi, the Italian ambassador in London, says he will never forget his first visit to an English pub. 'I asked the barmaid if I could have a quickie. I was mortified when the man next to me said: "The word is quiche, pronounced queesh"'.

Daily Telegraph

I saw a young woman wearing a T-shirt bearing the slogan: 'Practice safe sex – go fcuk yourself.' We deserve to be protected from language like this. When the word practise is used as a verb, it is spelled with an 's'.

Andrew Taylor, Knowl Hill, Berkshire.
Independent

'Ronking' means to smell badly, as in: 'Blimey, it ronks in here. Who farted?'

The Times

102 languages are spoken in East London.

Guardian

The ultimate citizenship exam for English people planning to move to Wales could be a test of their pronunciation of Llanfairpwllgwyngyllgogerychwyrndrobwllllantysliogogo goch. Rattling off the name could be an excellent way of overcoming Welsh fear of cultural domination by the English, according to a local government official in the Anglesey town. The name's sequence of 58 letters forms a Welsh pronunciation course in miniature, with almost all the usual difficulties condensed into one word. Visitors will be relieved to hear there are no plans to follow the example of 19th century Welsh nationalists, who are said to have extended Llanfairpwllgwyngyllgogerychwyrndrobwllllantysliog ogogoch's name to embarrass seekers after holiday cottages.

Guardian

The last person to speak only Cornish was Dolly Pentreath, who died in 1777. Her last words were: 'I will not speak English, you ugly black toad.'

Daily Telegraph

Call centre employees in India are trained to understand almost any regional UK dialect and to become familiar with British slang and obscenities. A special dictionary explains that: '"Rogering" is an act of sexual intercourse', but '"I'll be buggered" is merely an exclamation of surprise'.

Historian Paul Johnson wrote that nobody can be truly English until he can say 'Really' in 17 different ways.

Daily Mail

The National Canine Defence League changed its name to 'Dogs Trust' because too few people understood the word 'canine'.

Daily Mail

Barclays Bank has dug up more than 200 words for money in the English language. Top ten are: dosh, dough, readies, brass, bread, wad, lolly, wedge, wonga, moolah.

Sun

The United Kingdom? A *Times* letter saying that English is the language 'that God actually speaks' got a swift response from an Aberystwyth reader asking: 'Would He not have communication difficulties with the language of Heaven being Welsh?'

The Times

And a man from Powys was convicted of racially aggravated harassment after calling a Welsh woman English.

The Times

The Mexican Institute for Indigenous Languages fears for the future of the Zoque tongue. The only two people left alive to speak the language are two brothers who have fallen out and no longer talk to each other.

Independent on Sunday

Times master wordsmith Philip Howard rejects the old notion of prose as the selection of the best words, poetry as the best words in the best order and journalese as any old words in any old order.

The Times

Fear of the mother-in-law is: PENTHERAPHOBIA

The Times

CHAPTER 25
GOLDEN OLDIES

**The only entry in a cake contest wins
Second Prize...**

'On Friday, when he retired, Mr Reber was presented
with a portable TV and a pair of binoculars.'
  Essex Country Standard (from the *Guinness Book
of Humorous Gaffes*)

Edward Fuller, of Gillingham, Dorset, came across some
multi-nutrient tablets for people aged 65+. They were
labelled 'Do not take if you are pregnant or likely to
become pregnant.'

Daily Telegraph

'I still shave every morning using the rear-view
mirror of the last Spitfire I flew in World War II.'
Jack Feeney, Plymouth.

Guardian

BARMY BRITAIN

The revised Highway Code features a new section on powered wheelchairs. This follows a spate of accidents involving the elderly and disabled (nicknamed 'Hell's Grannies') driving in a reckless manner.

In 2004 seven were killed including a woman who reversed off a pier into the sea, and a man who was run over by a wheelchair painted in the colours of a Ferrari.

Sunday Times

An 84-year-old Weymouth man stepped out of the shower and water dripped from him onto his new bed. He tried to dry it with a hair dryer, but the mattress caught fire. He dragged the mattress into the porch, where it ignited a plastic gas pipe. This started a fire which burned down half of his roof and caused the evacuation of four nearby houses.

Guardian

I have heard that the four ages of man are: Lager, Aga, Saga and Gaga. Can anyone add a fifth?
Ron Stubbs, Maidstone, *Kent. Daily Telegraph*

The fifth age of man is Viagra, but I'm not sure if it goes after Lager and before Gaga. Hilary Stevens, Liskeard, Cornwall.

Daily Telegraph

Eileen Bridge, a 68-year-old love-struck grandmother from Accrington, Lancashire, beat hundreds of teenagers in a competition to find the nation's most poetic text message. She was runner up with an ode she wrote to her new husband:

Oh hart tht sorz
My luv adorz
He maks me give
Myslf 2 him
As my luv porz

Daily Telegraph

Visiting an old people's home in Florida, George Bush Senior once reportedly asked a resident: 'Do you know who I am?' The reply was: 'If you want to know who you are, you have to ask at reception.'

Observer

When my husband told a Saga holiday-going friend that Saga means Senile And Geriatric Association, she replied: 'Nonsense, it means Sex And Games for All'.

Dee Moss, Oxford. *Daily Telegraph*

Alex Baker, 96, has lived all his life in the house where he was born. The terraced house in Portsmouth, Hampshire, was bought some ten years before he was born for £130 and is now worth £130,000. There were two bedrooms upstairs and two rooms downstairs, plus a scullery and an outside toilet. There was a tin bath in the yard. The house has changed very little apart from an extension for a ground floor bathroom and Alex says: 'Why would I ever want to leave?'

His wife Edith, 86, says: 'Our key was always in the door and anybody who wanted to come in and have a cup of tea and a biscuit was always welcome.'

Alex says: 'We used to take our best shoes and clothes to the pawnbrokers on a Monday and get them back again on Friday.'

Daily Telegraph / Daily Mail

The NHS in Sunderland apologised to Joseph Dickinson for telling him to ensure a parent accompanied him to hospital. Joseph is 103.

Sunday Times

A wrinkly pop group called the Zimmers (with a combined age of over 3,000) shot into the UK's top 40 singles chart at number 26 in June 2007. It features Alf Carretta singing 'I hope I die before I get old'. Alf is 90.

Guardian

'A very good thing about getting old is that one can leave one's grandchildren when they start crying'. Norman Balon, landlord of Soho's Coach and Horse and known as the rudest publican in London, quoted in a collection of essays by famous oldies.

(*The Time of Your Life,* compiled by John Burningham.)

Independent

A *Times* reader asked: 'When does one become elderly?' The replies included:

'Middle age involves having to sit down to put on one's socks, whilst elderly demands a seated posture to put on one's underpants'. Simon Powell, London SW 11.

'When one's broad mind and narrow waist change places'. Frances Rentoul, Guildford, Surrey.

The Times

Ted Towle, 83, and Hilda Clarke, 73, from Nottingham, got married after living together for 49 years and producing nine children, 22 grandchildren, and 25 great-grandchildren.

Ted explained: 'Hilda won't be rushed into anything.'

Independent on Sunday

In June 2007, the UK's oldest triplets – Doris Kingston, Alice Holmes and Gladys Caress - celebrated their 80th birthday with a barbecue and a bouncy castle at Selby in North Yorkshire. They take their holidays together in Yorkshire resorts just up the road such as Whitby and Bridlington.

When they were born in 1927 their father was given a £1 note for each girl by George V.

Daily Telegraph

62-year-old grandmother Jenny Brown, of Wimblington, Cambridgeshire, was pleased when told that her Victoria sponge had won second prize in a village cake competition.

She was less pleased when she learned that it was the only entry.

Daily Mail

Firemen raced to an old folks' home in Hampshire after a smoke alarm was triggered by a pensioner warming slippers under a grill.

Independent on Sunday

Retirement no longer means slippers by the fire, knitting, reading and early to bed. A survey found that many intended to spice up retirement by embarking on extreme sports such as parachute jumping, bungee jumping, hang-gliding, swimming with dolphins and going on safari. And there were some who wanted to eat more cakes, grow a beard – and have more sex.

Daily Telegraph

The number of Britons reaching the age of 100 hit a record 9,000 in September 2007. The Daily Telegraph delved into 'The Secrets of the Centenarians' and quoted some of them:

Jean Underwood, of Bridport, Dorset, said: 'I have a nip of brandy in my coffee in the morning, no more than a teaspoon, unless I tip the bottle too heavy'.

Sarah Cooke, of Arnold, Nottingham, said that she had everything she needed 'apart from a 100-year-old man – or two 50-year-olds'.

Daily Telegraph

David Davidson, 79, and his wife Jean, 70, of Sheffield, stayed in a Travelodge in 1985 and liked it so much they moved in and have lived in one ever since. They even stay in Travelodges when they go on holiday. Said a Travelodge executive: 'We are going to rename their room The Davidsons' Suite and mount a plaque'.

Sun

Oh dear, what can the matter be? A 77-year-old lady spent 12 hours in a public lavatory in Pickering, North Yorkshire, when the caretaker locked up and went home. 'If I had had my mobile with me,' she said, 'I'd have been all right.'

Independent on Sunday

Friends of 100-year-old Phyllis Self believe she is the oldest boss in Britain. The great grandmother drives herself to her Whitehall Garden Centre in Wiltshire each day and says: 'I have no health secrets. I eat what I like and have a whisky and ginger in the evenings'.

Sun

Nora Hardwick, aged 102, got her kit off and posed nude for charity behind the bar of the Ermine Way pub in Ancaster, Lincolnshire. She said her children, aged 80, 74 and 62 'were very supportive'.

Sunday Telegraph

Harry Patch, of Wells, Somerset, the last surviving veteran to fight in the trenches during the First World War, celebrated his 109th birthday in June 2007. He served with the Duke of Cornwall's light infantry and fought at the Battle of Passchendaele, one of the bloodiest battles of the war. After blowing out the candles on his birthday cake Harry said: 'It's all a lot of fuss about nothing.'

Daily Telegraph

CHAPTER 26
JUST THE JOB

**A firm which supplies
Look-a-Likes has got seven Prince Harrys
and five Queen Elizabeths...**

In a learned leader T*he Times* gave this definition of an office a***hole: 'Someone who can instantly brighten a room by leaving it.'

The Times

Philip Habib complained to his bank about having to deal with call centres. He was told that the purpose of the call centre is to avoid having customers disturbing the routines of employees 'who have better things to do than talk to customers'.

Sunday Telegraph

The look-a-like industry goes from strength to strength. A girl who does Victoria Beckham can earn up to £4,000 a month, and one agency has got seven Prince Harrys and five Queen Elizabeths.

The Times

BARMY BRITAIN

Drusilla's Zoo Park in Alfriston, East Sussex, wanted a Fat Controller for its 'Thomas and Friends' railway (based on the children's books about Thomas the Tank Engine).

But the zoo was ordered not to specify that people applying for the job must be male and fat for fear of breaking anti-discrimination laws.

Said a zoo official: 'Theoretically, I could end up having to hire a thin woman.'

Daily Telegraph

Flaming June was flaming awful in 2007. The rain seemed to be incessant and went on and on into July, holding up Wimbledon, international cricket matches and other outdoor sports. But it had another unusual effect: the number of people who took 'sickies' fell by nearly a fifth.

A firm which analyses work attendance records said: 'Good weather is definitely the enemy of businesses. When the sun is shining we see a rise in people pulling a sickie'.

Daily Telegraph

Some 2.7million Britons claim to be too ill to work – suffering from disorders ranging from stress to varicose veins. Keith Waterhouse thought that most of us would have pitched the figure higher, the only surprise being that the official doing the counting was not off that day with a bad back.

Daily Mail

A survey reveals that a third of British workers think it is all right to 'pull a sickie'.

Top reason for taking a day off is a hangover. More than 50 per cent said they would be less likely to skive if their pay got docked.

Guardian

The Confederation of British Industry says bogus absences cost firms £11billion a year.

Sun

Postman Martin Calcutt, 31, of South Shields had to take sick leave after being bitten by his pet piranha.

The Times

Office staff spend more than 90 minutes a day gossiping, e-mailing friends and flirting.

Daily Telegraph

B. Hardy of Chester-le-Street, Durham, received an A4 envelope from a pension provider. It contained two A4 sheets of paper saying that they could not give him the information he required because the company 'works in a paperless environment'.

Sunday Telegraph

The Biggest Liar in the World Competition is held in Cumbria and dates back to the last century. Politicians and lawyers are banned on the grounds that they are professional liars.

Independent on Sunday

Scientists researching the best way to ventilate office buildings have come up with a radical solution – open the windows.

Financial Times

Don Snyder tells how he tackled the problem of employees abusing their allotted break time. He posted a notice saying: 'Starting immediately, your 15-minute breaks are being cut from a half hour to 20 minutes.'

Reader's Digest

23 per cent of photocopier faults are caused by people who sit on them to photocopy their buttocks.

Daily Star

My plumber's bill for half an hour's work was £100. I protested: 'I was a solicitor and couldn't charge at that rate.' He replied: 'I know. I couldn't either, when I was a solicitor.'

Daily Telegraph

A *Daily Telegraph* feature on the problems of giving references for unsatisfactory employees produced these suggestions from readers:

- My favourite is: 'I am sure he will join your company as he leaves ours – fired with enthusiasm.' Graham Hoyle, Shipley, West Yorkshire.

- A reference for a nurse said: 'She has shown herself capable of anything and we will be glad to see her back.' Dr Mark Cave, Abergavenny, Wales.

- A surgeon I worked for in North Wales preferred: 'This man informs me that he has been my house surgeon for six months. He has carried out all his duties to his entire satisfaction.' Dr John Griffiths, Anglesey.

- A ship's captain was once told: 'This man deserves a berth. Make sure you give him a wide one.' Brian Clifton, Wilmslow, Cheshire.

Daily Telegraph

Keith Sanderson lost the tip of his thumb in a factory guillotine in Newcastle – then cut off half of a finger demonstrating to his manager how it happened.

The Times

My wife was asked to retrieve an important document from the filing system of a fellow secretary who was off sick. After two hours of fruitless search she had to call the unfortunate girl at home to ask its whereabouts. The reply came back: 'I can't spell miscellaneous so I filed it under J for General'.

Norman Elwes, Chelmsford. *The Times*

CHAPTER 27

CHRISTMAS PRESENCE

Standing under mistletoe can lead to unexpected pregnancy...

To get the job done on Christmas Eve, Santa Claus has to travel 221 million miles at an average speed of 1,279 miles per second, 6,395 times the speed of sound.

Daily Telegraph

Mrs Janice Stone, of Hull, tells of children singing carols at the local old folks' home. 'A friend's four year old grandson was asked if the oldsters had enjoyed the carols.

"Yes", he replied. "Except for the dead one at the front"'.

Daily Mail

The five-year-old grandson of Mrs Lesley Mills of Wolverhampton was one of the three kings in his school's nativity play. She asked him what he had given to Jesus - gold, frankincense or myrrh. The boy said he didn't know, but the box looked like a McDonald's Happy Meal.

Daily Mail

Instead of baubles, the Tate Britain's Christmas tree featured models of cherubs complete with explicit depictions of their private parts.

Daily Mail

The *Sunday Times* had some fun with a whole page headlined MERRY CHRISTMAS... FROM ELF AND SAFETY. Among the hilarious pieces of advice were these two:

- If you have a fairy at the top of your tree you should be aware that the word 'fairy' can cause offence. A more appropriate term would be 'wand bearer'.
- Do not stand under mistletoe as it can lead to unexpected pregnancy.

Sunday Times

The 2006 Christmas card from the Commission for Racial Equality features a nativity scene and is presented as a draft upon which politically correct comments have been scribbled. Such as:

- The snow looks hideously white.
- The animals pulling the sleigh should be product of equal opportunities employment policies, not all one species.
- Stable not compliant with housing code – where is disabled access?
- Sheep should look more diverse.
- Three Wise Men can't be all men.

Daily Mail

The Bishop of Southwark denied being drunk during an incident in which he lost his belongings and suffered head injuries after a 2006 Christmas party at the Irish Embassy in London (*Times Online*).

Earlier a Times leader told its readers that the annual party at the Irish Embassy had a reputation for hospitality so generous that 'guests have been known to cling to the pavement all the way home for fear of falling off'.

The Times

The *Telegraph*'s cartoonist Matt had a wife telling her husband: 'They must have been men – they followed a star rather than stop and ask directions.'

Daily Telegraph

The Royal Christmas lunch is a brief, glum affair at Sandringham. From start to finish, the record is 50 minutes. Perhaps the reason why the lunch is so brief is that the Royal Family, just like other families, 'can only take so much of each other at Christmas'.

Daily Mail

Carmarthenshire banned its taxi drivers from wearing Santa Claus outfits 'because they must always resemble their identity card pictures'.

Guardian

It's the ultimate Christmas gift for men – a new Giant Swiss Army knife which has 85 devices, weighs 2lb and costs nearly £500. Its devices include:

- A golf club face cleaner.
- Fish hook disgorger.
- Cigar cutter.
- Flashlight.
- Magnifying glass with screwdriver.
- Can opener.
- Adjustable pliers.
- Flat nose pliers.
- Needle nosed pliers with wire cutter.
- Phillips screwdriver.
- Metal file.
- Round needle file.
- Compass.
- Ruler.
- Scissors.
- Allen wrench.
- Allen key.
- Bottle top lifter.
- Tyre gauge.
- 2.5inch knife blade.

It does not, however, have a device for getting stones out of horses' hooves. This is, apparently, mythological.

When Chris Bonnington headed a Himalayan expedition in 1970 he used every blade in his Swiss Army knife except the fish scaler. He apologised for this, explaining that there are no fish on the south face of Annapurna.

Guardian

The *Sunday Telegraph* called this 'the shaggiest, most unbelievable Christmas story of all':

At Santa's Magical Animal Kingdom in Westmeath, Ireland, staff were looking forward to their Christmas feast – but someone forgot to secure the pen of their Bactrian camel Gus. This immense, shaggy, intimidating Ship of the Desert escaped and headed for the festive table. Gus is described as 'about the size of a small elephant with large yellow, prominent front teeth'. By the time staff turned up for their party Gus had scoffed more than 200 mince pies and all the crisps and sandwiches and was on his sixth can of Guinness.

Trapeze artist Amanda Sandow said: 'The mess was appalling. It was like a bomb had gone off. He'd eaten the lot. We were pretty angry at the time, but we soon forgave him. He's a lovable rogue and who can blame him for celebrating Christmas.'

How does a camel open a can of Guinness? 'With no bother at all', said 14-year-old Clodagh Cleary. 'He was biting the tops off with his big strong teeth and sucking up the Guinness. It was brilliant.'

Kate Kiernan said: 'Sandwiches for 20 people and 200 mince pies would be nothing for him. It must all go in his humps, we reckon.'

Sunday Telegraph

Scrooge is alive, if not very well. He was out and about grizzling 'Bah! Humbug!' across the nation in the run up to the 2006 festive season:

- A survey of 23,000 employers revealed that 74% banned Xmas decorations because of fears that followers of other faiths might be upset. *Sun*

- Actors at a Preston pantomime were banned from throwing sweets to children in the audience. *Daily Mail*

- A Santa was prevented from touring Leighton Buzzard, Bedfordshire, because his sleigh did not have a seat belt. The town's Round Table have been towing Santa around in a float for 45 years. *Sun*

- For the first time in 250 years, children will not be allowed to carry candles at Chelmsford Cathedral's Christingle service in case their hair catches fire. There is no record of this happening since the services began in 1747. *Daily Telegraph*

- Villagers in Embsay, North Yorkshire, were told that their festive party would be cancelled unless they carried out a 'risk assessment' on mince pies made by the Women's Institute. *Sun*

- For 40 years the Torbay Gospelaires sang carols in the wards of their local hospital. In 2006 they were banned from the wards for fear of infection.

Daily Telegraph

Trust the Irish to cock a snoot at Scrooges. Children there often put out sacks instead of socks for Santa to fill. It is traditional to leave out mince pies and a bottle of Guinness for the old fellow.

The Times

Stuart Prebble, creator of TV's Grumpy Old Men series, has a grumpy old look at Christmas and says of pantomimes that in the good old days they were aimed at kids and were full of silly jokes and slapstick.

'Now they're all sex, smut and double entendres. Even the phrase "He's behind you" carries a whole different meaning.'

From a *Daily Mail* selection of Prebble's seasonal bleatings in his book *Grumpy Old Christmas* (Weidenfeld & Nicholson, £9.99).

A *Daily Telegraph* reader remembered receiving a Christmas gift from the Mayor of Stalybridge during World War II. It contained a jar of Brylcreem and a packet of razor blades.

'I was in the Women's Auxiliary Service,' writes Joan Brown of Bowness-on-Windermere, Cumbria.

Daily Telegraph

Have a merry festive season and don't read this. The Royal Society for the Prevention of Accidents reports that:

- More than 6,000 people will end up in hospital on Christmas day.
- During the 12 days of Christmas more than 80,000 will visit A&E wards.

There will be:

- Drunken dads severing fingers while trying to carve the turkey.
- Chefs not following the correct lifting procedure when moving 24lb turkeys.
- Christmas trees causing more than 1,000 injuries (branches in eyes and falling off chairs reaching to put the fairy on top).
- Fires caused by lighting candles on Christmas trees and positioning candles underneath strings of cards.
- Heavy gifts hidden on top of wardrobes falling off and causing head injuries.
- Screwdrivers driven through the palm while trying to penetrate packaging.
- Knives slashing through flesh while cutting through thick layers of sticky tape.

Guardian G2

The Santa Claus working in Paisley's shopping centre near Glasgow was forced to swap his red hat for a hard hat after being bombarded with mince pies by youths.

Guardian

In the run-up to the festive season newspapers and magazines vie with each other to provide alleged hangover cures, old and new.

The Daily Telegraph magazine filled a page under the headline: 'Are there hangover cures that actually work?' It listed five 'hangover helpers' ranging in price from £4.99 (RU 21 tablets) to £15.39 (Planetary Herbal Kudzu Complex capsules), and ended up with a last paragraph quoting an expert whose research concluded that 'there was not a lot of evidence for cures... In the end, nothing can prevent or treat hangovers – the only thing is not to drink.'

Daily Telegraph magazine. (Sorry. Merry Christmas and a Happy New Year anyway.)

For Andy Park, 45, of Wiltshire, it is Christmas every day – starting with mince pies and turkey sandwiches for breakfast, crackers at lunch and a video of the Queen's Speech at 3pm and a roast turkey dinner. He has been doing this for 12 years and has consumed an estimated 4,380 turkeys.

Independent on Sunday

The average Christmas tree is home to 30,000 bugs, including spiders, fleas and lice.

Reader's Digest

Simon Hoggart's Saturday column in the *Guardian* has been delving into Christmas catalogues and finding such essentials as:

- An easy-clean fibreglass Petstep (£67.50) — a gangplank to allow dogs to stroll into the car boot without having to be lifted onto the protective blanket.
- Battery powered insole heaters (£72.95).
- A Self-Stirring Mug (£10.95).

But Simon hadn't realised how long Christmas catalogues have been around until Robin Dow wrote from Sheffield about a Victorian version which offered a walking cane that converted into a small step-ladder in case the owner met a mad dog.

Guardian

Kelvin MacKenzie reports on The Four Stages of Father Christmas:
1. You believe in Father Christmas
2. You don't believe in Father Christmas
3. You are Father Christmas
4. You look like Father Christmas

Sun

A survey revealed that one of the reasons why pubs are so popular at Christmas is that people go there to escape the in-laws.

Sun

The gags in Christmas crackers are normally so bad that everyone laughs at the stupidity of them. Here are some of the worst of the 2007 vintage:

- What is Santa's favourite pizza? One that's deep pan, crisp and even.
- On which side do chickens have most feathers? The outside.
- What's furry and minty. A polo bear.
- Who hides in the bakery at Christmas? A mince spy.
- What do you call a penguin in the Sahara desert? Lost.

Daily Telegraph

In order to get airborne, Father Christmas's reindeer would need wings ten metres (33ft) long according to the calculations of Paolo Viscardi, a flight physiologist at the University of Leeds. He worked out that Rudolph & Co would need a total wing area of at least nine square metres.

Guardian

Receiving a Christmas card with a robin on it is a sign of something nasty to come according to the *Penguin Guide to the Superstitions of Britain and Ireland*. But wearing a spider in a bag around your neck until it dies will bring good luck.

Daily Mail

Asda supermarket held a contest to find new jokes for Christmas crackers saying: 'Groaning at awful cracker jokes is part of the Christmas fun. The aim was to not to introduce good jokes, but to bring in new bad ones'. These are some of the winners:

- What are chiropodists' favourite crisps? Cheese and bunion.
- Why did the man take his budgie to the bookies? So that it could have a flutter.
- What do you do with a sick bee? Take it to the waspital.
- What did the liver say to the kidney after a night out? 'I feel offal'.
- What is red, white and blue and flaps in a tree? A Union Jackdaw.

Daily Mail

A Chippenham couple celebrated Christmas 2007 with the world's oldest imitation tree. The 120 year-old miniature cost 6d (that's two and a half p) and has been handed down in the family since 1886. 'It amazes me to think that it has been appearing every Christmas since Victorian times. We will be passing it on to our son', says Janet Parker.

The Times

Forget the turkey. In parts of the Outer Hebrides the Christmas bird of choice is the guga (or baby gannet). This unusual festive seabird is a highly-prized delicacy and some are sent around the world to expatriates. Traditionally eaten with boiled potatoes and no trimmings, preparation involves scrubbing off the salt and soaking overnight. Old hands suggest cooking the guga outdoors 'because of the dreadful smell'. It is said to taste like a cross between duck and mackerel.

Daily Telegraph

CHAPTER 28

ODDS AND SODS

Clement Attlee is a modest man who has much to be modest about...

The Pentagon once considered developing a weapon that would cause flatulence. It was to be called the 'Who? Me?' device.

Reader's Digest

John Murrell, of Cambridge, was astonished when a bank turned him down because he exceeded their maximum age limit. And even more astonished by a letter saying that he could reapply '...should your circumstances change in the next six months'.

The Times

D. Kehoe, of Clayton-le-Moors, Lancashire spotted in a letter from the Post Office:

'When we closed your account the balance was £0.00. We will look after this for you until you claim it'.

Daily Mail

Daily Telegraph readers complained about people not sending thank you letters and David Greenway, of Andover, Hampshire wrote about his grandmother: 'She would send half a ten shilling note, and only when you had written to thank her did you get the other half'.

Daily Telegraph

Some of the strange requests for money received by the National Lottery:
• To respray a Cortina
• Buy a pub
• Set up a dinosaur farm
• Publish evidence to prove Einstein and Isaac Newton were wrong

Independent on Sunday

Noël Coward wrote to one of his critics: 'Sir, I am seated in the smallest room in the house. Your review is in front of me. In a moment it will be behind me.'

Independent

Homer Simpson, pot-bellied head of America's most dysfunctional family, has made it into the *Oxford Dictionary of Modern Quotations* – alongside such literary luminaries as George Bernard Shaw and Oscar Wilde. One of his chosen quotes:

'Kids, you tried your best and you failed miserably. The lesson is never try.'

Sun

Joan Rivers was in caustic form at the finals of Miss Great Britain. 'It's not just about surface beauty. We've got 50 girls here. Two of them even know their names'.

Asked for beauty tips she said: 'Wear a really heavy bag over your face. The older you get the longer the bag has to get.'

The Times

People from Cork have a reputation of looking upon themselves as superior to their fellow countrymen, and have been subjected to a *Book of Corkmen Jokes*. (By Des McHale, Mercier Press). It opens with:

A Corkman reported his car stolen and the police asked if he had got a good look at the thief.

'No', said the Corkman, 'but I've got his number'.

The Times

Every month the UK Intellectual Property Office receives around 500 inventions, and the Daily Telegraph reports on some wacky ones:

- A contraption to facilitate the birth of a child by centrifugal force. The mother-to-be is strapped to a table that spins around at high speed. The baby is forced out and caught in a net.
- A ladder to let spiders climb out of the bath.
- An airman's helmet with fitted pop-up parachute.
- A cat flap with a colour sensor which would admit the designer's ginger tom, but block the passage of his neighbour's black moggie.

Daily Telegraph

James Bond actor Daniel Craig was asked what it was like being an international star.

He replied: 'Well, I get to hang around with all the best women, drive the fastest cars, travel in speedboats and private jets, sleep in the best hotels and have beautiful women pursuing me from all over the world... It's absolutely bloody awful.'

Daily Mail

My friend's four-year-old girl announced very loudly at the ballet: 'Look Mum, that man is hiding his sweeties where I hide mine.'

Mrs. S. Smith, Uxbridge. *Daily Mail*

Guardian diarist Jon Henley reports on two impressive toilet seats:

- The Kohler C3 which has cleansing wands, heated seat with three temperature settings, warm air fan, lighted bowl, deodorizer, Quiet-Close seat and full remote control.
- The Clean Seat Matic with Automatic Infrared-Activated Voice Chip, which not only lines itself with paper but reminds users to flush it and broadcasts up to three minutes of advertisements.

Guardian

During the Dunkirk retreat Major General Lord Burnham encountered his son on the beach. He greeted him with: 'I see you failed to shave this morning'.

W. F. Deedes in the *Daily Telegraph*

At the height of a gale, the harbourmaster radioed a coastguard and asked him to estimate the wind speed. He replied he was sorry, but he didn't have a gauge. However, if it was any help, the wind had just blown his Land Rover off the cliff.

Aberdeen Evening Express / BBC News Quiz

Commenting on a complaint from a Mr Arthur Purdey about a large gas bill, a spokesman for North West Gas said, 'We agree it was rather high for the time of year. It's possible Mr Purdey has been charged for the gas used up during the explosion that destroyed his house.'

Daily Telegraph / BBC News Quiz

A young girl who was blown out to sea on a set of inflatable teeth was rescued by a man on an inflatable lobster. A coastguard spokesman commented, 'This sort of thing is all too common'.

The Times

If you are pleasantly surprised at being able to squeeze into 32inch waist jeans – don't celebrate too soon. Some fashion companies flatter their customers – both men and women – by understating the true waistline.

Example: jeans claiming to be a slim-fit 30 can be actually 36. It's known as 'vanity sizing'.

Daily Mail

While we are being urged to help save the planet by turning off the TV standby, Les Deakin, of Warrington, writes: 'What about the rest? There is the microwave, oven clock, refrigerator, freezer, burglar alarm, doorbell, computer, bedroom TV, DVD, Freeserve box, porch light, central heating controller, radio alarm clock and the Economy 7 timer'.

Mr Deakin feels that by the time you have gone round switching them all off, it could well be time to get up and put them on again.

The Times

The Bulwer-Lytton Fiction Prize (awarded for deliberately bad writing) is named after the author who began his novel with the immortal words 'It was a dark and stormy night'. The 2007 winner of the Adventure Category was:

'As the hippo's jaws clamped on Henry's body he noted its teeth were badly in need of a clean, preferably with one of those electric sonic tooth-brushes, and he reflected that his name would be immortalised by his unusual death, since hippo killings are not a daily occurrence, at least not in the high street of Chipping Sodbury.'
Tim Lafferty, Woking, Surrey.

Independent on Sunday

It's a myth that women are chatterboxes who never let a man get a word in edgeways. The most prolific talker during a series of tests was a man who yakked his way through 47,000 words a day. The most effusive woman managed a mere 40,000.

- David Beckham speaks at 174 words a minute.
- Dame Helen Mirren – 153 words a minute.
- Peter O'Sullivan, racing commentator – 238.
- JK Rowling – 169.
- Churchill spoke at 111 words a minute.

The Times

The organisers of the Two Moors music festival in Devon spent two years raising £26,000 to buy a Bosendorfer piano – which is to a pianist what a Stradivarius is to a string player. But, when being unloaded from its lorry, the piano slipped and crashed 8ft down an embankment.

The noise made by the falling Rolls-Royce of grand pianos was described as being like 'ten honky tonk pianos being hit by mallets'.

The Times, Telegraph, Mail, Guardian

Rock singer and millionaire green queen Sheryl Crow wants us to save the planet by using only one sheet of toilet paper per visit to the loo.

Jan Moir explodes: 'One! Quite how this diktat is to be policed is anyone's guess.'

Daily Telegraph

To help save the planet from free plastic bags Sainsbury's offered an iconic 'I'm Not A Plastic Bag' bag. Rachel Thomas, of Tunbridge Wells, queued up to get hers and the lady at the checkout kindly put it in a plastic carrier bag and wished her a good day.

The Times

In May 2007 the *Daily Telegraph* celebrated the 100th anniversary of the birth of John Wayne, who embodies almost everything Hollywood now considers politically incorrect – a tough talking, red-blooded man's man, pro-war patriot and, in his own words, a 'right wing conservative extremist'. His real name was Marion Robert Morrison and his quotes include:

'A man's godda do what a man's godda do'

'Women have the right to work wherever they want as long as they have the dinner ready when you get home'.

Daily Telegraph

When the Cutty Sark was ravaged by fire at Greenwich in May 2007 every paper carried pages and pages of the clipper's glorious history from the moment it slid into the Clyde in 1869. The Times recorded how she was a modern vessel in her day. 'She had lavatories at a time when answering a call of nature was usually done by squatting over the ship's side.'

The Times

In August 2007 a postcard was delivered to Anthony Ely, of Winthorpe, Lincolnshire, along with an apology for delay. It was posted in August 1908.

The Times

Sherwood Forest was astir when it was revealed that a blockbuster film was being made portraying the Sheriff of Nottingham as a good guy trying to keep the peace while Robin Hood was just some young thug in a Lincoln-green hoodie.

The *Guardian* harrumphed: 'Robin a baddie? Lay off our legend, Hollywood.'

Guardian

In 1997 David Ashcroft won £12.3 million on the National Lottery and he said at the time that his win would not change his way of life.

Ten years later the Daily Mail reported that David, 40, still lives in the same three bedroom terraced house in Liverpool with his parents. He still works as a furniture restorer – the job he trained for as a teenager. But he did buy a new van, double glazed the family home, and has a caravan in North Wales where they go on holiday. He has never travelled abroad, does not drink or smoke – but has the occasional cream cake.

Daily Mail

In June 2007 London celebrated the 200th anniversary of the arrival of street gas lamps. Lamp attendant Martin Caulfield was there lighting a lamp near Big Ben wearing a traditional bowler hat. He is one of London's six lamplighters still on the job.

Daily Telegraph

A survey revealed some of the oddball items left behind in hotel rooms:
- A stuffed crocodile
- A wooden leg
- A pet dog
- A racing bike worth £19,000

The survey did not reveal why a carrot found in a bed was wrapped in cling film.

Independent on Sunday

A newly unearthed copy of a 1694 volume entitled *The Ladies Dictionary – Being a General Entertainment of the Fair Sex*, is described as a virtual Cosmopolitan of its time. It dismisses thin women as 'scragged, sad-looking and not comely' and says 'a painted face is enough to destroy the reputation of her that uses it'.

The Times

Angela Kenny, of East Kilbride, Scotland – Britain's biggest Lottery winner – went shopping soon after picking up £35.4 million... At a discount centre which slashes prices on brand names and sells cheap seconds.

Sun

A 51-year-old amateur sailor from Newquay, Cornwall, capsized his catamaran dozens of times, costing the RNLI thousands of pounds in rescue missions.

His boat was called Mischief and the RNLI called him Captain Calamity.

They advised the accident prone enthusiast to find a new hobby.

Daily Telegraph

Owen Jenkins, of Lowestoft, Suffolk, writes about arriving with a small band of sailors at Cork railway station on a Saturday night soon after the Second World War. They asked for the time of the last train to Cobh and a guard said:

'Well now, about what time would you lads be wanting to go?'

'About half-past nine', they replied.

'Right then. Come and tell me when you are all aboard and then we'll be off.'

The Times

Actress Sienna Miller discussed her eco-credentials and said: 'It's impossible in my industry to not travel... I don't think I can stop flying at the moment, but I can start having less baths.'

Independent on Sunday

The World Series of Poker rolled into London town in September 2007 and one of the top guns let it be known that he can cut a carrot in half by flicking a playing card at it.

The Times

A whole lotta faking going on. There are 80,000 Elvis Presley impersonators worldwide. When the BBC began a search for the best, Broadcasting House was seething with Elvises: tall, short, macho, weedy, adolescent, and 'old enough to know better'.

Daily Mail Weekend magazine

At a time when Captain Alexander Stewart was fighting in the World War I trenches, officialdom wanted to know how many pairs of socks his company had. When he replied that there were 141 and a half there was an immediate memo demanding to know at once, 'How you come to be deficient of one sock?' He replied: 'Man lost his leg.'

Guardian

The *Penny Pincher's Book*, by John and Irma Mustoe, is described in the Daily Mail as 'a cult guide for 21st century misers'. Among its recommendations:

• Turn old rubber gloves into elastic bands
• Keep candles in the fridge to make them burn slower
• Use a pepper shaker for olive oil – it releases less than pouring from a bottle
• Chew beeswax instead of expensive nicotine gums
• Buy anti-freeze in the summer when it is cheaper
• Never go to a supermarket on an empty stomach because hungry shoppers are more likely to snap up expensive sweets and snacks
• Re-use junk mail envelopes by turning them inside out then glue the edges
• Wash your hands in cold water
• Cut Brillo pads, nylon scourers, dusters and sponges in half

Daily Mail

The Ig Nobel awards for ludicrous investigations are produced by a science humour magazine called *Annals of Improbable Research*. In 2007 the language prize went to Barcelona University for proving that rats cannot tell the difference between Japanese being spoken backwards and Dutch being spoken backwards. The biology prize went to a Brit, Brian Whitcomb, who established that amateur sword-swallowers are subject to sore throats.

Independent

Barcelona was also the scene of an 'inspiring act of endurance, courage and accomplishment' when Britain's Wayne Iles blew through a straw and sent a Malteser a world-record distance of 11ft 0.2inches.

Independent on Sunday (from the *Guinness Book of Records*)

Noël Coward took a taxi from the Savoy to the Dorchester and his driver grumbled about picking up a fare for such a short trip. Noël paid the five shillings fare and gave a £20 tip saying: 'If you had been more polite you would have received my usual tip'.

The Times

Chris Harding, of Parkstone, Dorset, was advised that the best way to tip a ship's steward was to give him a bank note torn in half. If he got satisfaction the steward got the other half at the end of the journey.

The Times

Millionaire Nubar Gulbenkian reputedly put a ten shilling note on the table when sitting down to dine in a restaurant, telling the waiter: 'Yours if I'm satisfied, mine if I'm not.'

David Sinclair, Isington, Hampshire. *The Times*

Following the Gulbenkian tipping story, Mike Mitchell, of Hove, Sussex, wrote: I think it was the same gentleman who scorned luxury limousines and chose a traditional London taxi, boasting that 'It can turn on a sixpence – whatever that is'.

The Times

In January 1992 a container was washed off a cargo ship – releasing thousands of plastic toy ducks into the Pacific Ocean. In June 2007 The Times reported: 'A flotilla of plastic ducks is heading for British beaches... after journeying nearly 17,000 miles.' Two children's books have been written about the saga and the ducks have become collector's items, changing hands for £500.

The Times

Alan Jenkins, of Port Talbot, Glamorgan, had a tattoo of his girlfriend's face on his back, but, after 15 years, they split up. Philosophically, Alan said 'I've got some room on my chest if I get hooked up again.'

Sunday Times / Daily Mirror

At the last count, 12,682 designs for toothbrushes had been lodged at the patents office.

Daily Telegraph

A survey of wit by the digital TV channel Dave produced these examples:

- 'I have nothing to declare except my genius' (Oscar Wilde)
- 'Clement Attlee is a modest man who has much to be modest about' (Winston Churchill)
- 'Maids want nothing but husbands, and when they have them, they want everything' (William Shakespeare)
- 'I wouldn't say I was the best manager in the business. But I was in the top one' (Brian Clough)

57% of those surveyed thought that men are wittier then women – and there were no female entries in the top ten.

Daily Mail

When NASA started sending astronauts into space they realised that ball point pens would not work at zero gravity. A multi-dollar investment and two years of tests resulted in a pen that could write upside down on almost any surface and at any temperature from below freezing to over 300°C. When confronted by the same problem the Russians used a pencil.

Bureau Direct sales brochure

Despite the fact that George Washington said he would never set foot in England, there is a monument to the great man in Trafalgar Square. It rests on a base of American soil especially sent over. Unfortunately, the lawns there have become a day-long resting place for alcoholics, drug addicts and tramps.

Daily Telegraph

Heidi Lebers, 39, from East Sussex, celebrated New Year by releasing a balloon bearing the message 'Happy New Year to whoever finds this'. Six weeks later she got a letter from Toucy in France telling her off for littering up the place.

The Times

Lord Berners, the composer, made sure that if other passengers got into his railway carriage they soon left. He would take his temperature anally every five minutes with a large clinical thermometer.

Independent – from a review of *Brewer's Rogues, Villains and Eccentrics* by William Donaldson.

**The Publishers wish to acknowledge
the following publications**

Daily Mail
Daily Express
The Times
Daily Telegraph
Sun
Guardian
Financial Times
Independent
Scotsman
Metro
News of the World
Independent on Sunday
Sunday Telegraph
Observer Magazine
Observer Food Magazine (*OFM*)
Sunday Mercury

London Review of Books
The Press Gazette
Reader's Digest
Catholic Herald.
Private Eye
Economist
Yorkshire Post
Birmingham Evening Mail
Newcastle Advertiser
Newcastle Evening Chronicle
Liverpool Daily Post
Evening Post, Leeds
Sheffield General Cemetery Trust Magazine
Brighton Argus
Coventry Evening Telegraph
Colchester Evening Gazette
Tamworth Times
Halifax Courier
Henley Standard
West Sussex Gazette
Western Morning News
Western Mail
Oban Times
Eastbourne & District Advertiser
Seaford Friday Ad
Cumberland News
Scunthorpe Target
Shropshire Star
Tandridge Chronicle
Radio Times

New Scientist
Country Life
BBC Olive magazine
Journal of Sexual Medicine
Adult Learners' Week
Focus magazine
Cambria magazine
Dogs Today
BBC News
Surrey Online
Teletext